Essentials of Washinkai Karate

Christopher Thompson

ACKNOWLEDGEMENTS

England
Graham Hiscock — Photography
Alison Thompson — Typing
Paul Hacker — Photographic Editor

Japan
Takao Yamamoto — Sensei
Takeshi Sasaki — Kancho
Chido-Kan Karate Do

DEDICATION

I dedicate this book to my parents who constantly encouraged me to train hard.

First published in 2015 by BTKA publishing,
a division of The British Traditional Karate Association.

Based upon 'Essentials of Wado-ryu' by Chris Thompson, 1988.

To contact BTKA Publishing please email
cthompson1@btconnect.com

© Chris Thompson
Design by Paul Hacker

All rights reserved. No part of this publication may be reproduced, or transmitted in any form or by any means, electronic or mechanical including photocopying, recording, or by any information storage or retrieval system, without the prior written permission of the copyright owners.

The moral right of the author has been asserted

First edition

Paperback Edition ISBN 978-0-9933891-0-8

Table of Contents

Short history of karate 8
The major styles of karate-do 18
History of Wado-Ryu 22
Short history of Christopher Thompson and Washinkai Karate-Do Renmei 28
Calisthenics 34
Kihon (Basics) 40
Kata 66
Yakusoku Kumite 104
Ji-Yu Kumite 134
The name Wado Ryu 138
Afterword
Appendix of kata variations 144

Special thanks to
Neville Smith (7th Dan), who did all the pair work and
Paul Hacker (5th Dan) for his help in completing this book.

PREFACE

Karate is the art of unarmed combat using parts of the body as weapons: hands, feet, elbows and knees. It is also an exciting sport providing a most fascinating and exhilarating challenge for anyone taking it up, regardless of age. Through systematic and prolonged training, mental as well as physical, over many years, one can become proficient at the art.

It was in 1969 that I first donned a do-gi (karate suit). In that short period of time there have been many great improvements in the art of karate, not only in competition, but also in its tuition. Karate technique has also evolved and the karate-ka, a practitioner, is armed with a greater repertoire of technique.

At the time I started karate, students of many clubs literally did as they were told, regardless of whether the exercises or techniques performed were detrimental to their health. If one had a Japanese instructor, the chances were that when ji-yu kumite (sparring) commenced, you would be in for a battering should you be unfortunate enough to be chosen by him.

This would not be tolerated in today's climate. People are more aware of their rights and legal action would be taken against any belligerent instructor. Karate clubs would not survive and an instructor could never earn a living through a shrinking membership. There is nothing wrong with a student questioning his instructor as to why he is carrying out a certain technique and I believe it should be encouraged. This, unfortunately, was not the way in the early days of karate in this country. Therefore anybody presently teaching karate has a huge responsibility to his students, not only in the dojo (training area), but also outside, as his actions are often under scrutiny.

The majority of good instructors nowadays have a sound knowledge of the body's anatomy and when carrying out exercises, especially stretching, ensure that they are done in a scientific manner. The more conscientious instructor takes his role one step further by becoming a qualified First Aider.

The most important change since karate came to this country is the total acceptance of insurance linked to karate. The majority of karate associations and governing bodies have schemes which cover all their membership. In my opinion, this has allowed students to fully commit themselves in their training and have peace of mind that should they sustain an injury then some form of compensation for loss of earnings would be made available.

I have been extremely fortunate in having travelled abroad extensively and been able to train with many senior instructors of various schools of karate. The knowledge I have gained has helped me compile this book.

My aims for writing this book are to show the student of Wado-Ryu Karate, no matter what level, the correct ways of carrying out exercises, executing kicks, punches and strikes (kihon) which make up many of the syllabuses of Japanese Wado-Ryu Karate-do. Additionally, there are many Yakusoku-kumite (pairs) shown in the Ippon-kumite form (one-step sparring), demonstrating counters against punches and kicks being delivered to different parts of the body. The extensive use of Tai-sabaki (hip shift) can be seen throughout. The founder of Wado-Ryu was instrumental in introducing this manoeuvre into karate. The five Pinan Kata are also shown and I have tried to show them in their near original form as created by Anko Itosu at the turn of the 20th Century. The book will be invaluable to students of my own organisation, Washinkai Karate-Do Renmei, who will find all of the techniques in their syllabus covered here.

 **PREFACE**

Written in 1988

I have been involved in the martial arts for over 50 years, establishing one of the earliest full-time judo clubs "The Judokan" in this country in 1954. I introduced Wado Ryu Karate into the Club in 1965. I remember Chris Thompson starting at the club nearly 20 years ago as an enthusiastic teenager. His continuous training in karate was rewarded by receiving his Shodan in just two years.

Throughout the 1970s I watched Chris Thompson's karate develop to a high standard. As he matured and began teaching for me, I realised he not only understood the techniques he was performing, but was able to convey his knowledge to students no matter what their ability or grade.

With his extensive travel, he has managed to train with many karate masters throughout the world. His ability and understanding of karate-do has enabled him to build a large, loyal following of karate students in this country.

I am sure this book will give you an insight into some of the knowledge that the author has amassed on the Wado-Ryu style of karate.

Percy Sekine (1920 – 2010)
7th Dan Kodokan Japan
Former International
Former British Team Manager

Chris Thompson with Teruo Hayashi

CHAPTER 1

Short History of Karate

There are many good books available covering the history of karate in great depth from its very early beginnings. Documented evidence of systemised fighting can be traced as far back as 4,000 BC when the Egyptian military carved hieroglyphics onto the walls of the Pyramids depicting fighting scenes. A systemised form of unarmed combat was used in the early Greek Olympic Games, where fights often resulted in death. China's advanced civilisation also had a systemised form of military fighting whilst the rest of the known world still lived in caves.

Eastern History

Bodhidharma, a Buddhist monk and supposed reincarnation of Buddha, travelled from India to China in approximately AD 550, settling at the Shaolin Temple where he is accredited with introducing exercises that are the foundation of today's modern karate.
Unfortunately, there does tend to be some discrepancies with dates of the last few hundred years and so I will give a short history of karate from the end of the last century to the present day where the facts are documented and indisputable.

Okinawa

Okinawa is one of the largest of the Ryukyu Islands, which are based at the southern tip of Japan and lie due east of China, equidistant to both countries. It has not only had its loyalties divided throughout the centuries, but also had both Japan and China trying to colonise the island. Its very location also led to it becoming an important trading post for all countries of the

Far East which were unable to trade directly with each other. The Island became a haven for seamen of different nationalities who, by the very nature of their profession, were very tough and hardened men. They frequently exchanged their own peculiar fighting methods with one another in a friendly atmosphere, often whilst drinking, but it was not uncommon for techniques to be exchanged in real combat. The Okinawans, using all this invaluable knowledge, formed their own eclectic fighting system.

In the 15th and 16th Centuries, Chinese military attaches were based in Okinawa as the two countries then had very strong ties. In the early 17th Century, the Satsuma clan of Japan invaded Okinawa, forcing the islanders to capitulate within several weeks. Okinawa was now in effect a colony under the direct rule of the Japanese. The normal daily routine of the Okinawans was uninterrupted. However, all weapons were confiscated, making the islanders totally subservient. The Okinawans' link with China was not severed and Chinese military attaches were still allowed on the island. 'Kushanku' and 'Chinto', two of these attaches (who are to this day remembered in karate kata – forms), were experts in the martial arts, and together with many others, in secret taught the Okinawans a form of Chinese combat: Ch'uan-fa ('Chinese fist-way').

As previously mentioned, the Okinawans had developed a fighting system of their own, using all parts of their bodies, which was generally known as 'Okinawan Te' or 'To-de'. Although very secretive, many began to study the art at an early age from immediate members of the family or very close friends. A stranger had very little chance of learning the system of Okinawan-Te. The towns of Shuri, Tomari and Naha had created their own peculiar forms of Okinawan Te, hence Shuri-te, Tomari-te and Naha-te. 'Te' meaning 'hand'. Naha-te and Tomari-te later became Shorei-ryu, a school teaching hard, strong and powerful techniques, whilst Shuri-te became Shorin-ryu, concentrating on a faster execution of technique with emphasis on speed, rather than strength. Therefore over the centuries, through visiting Chinese military attaches, monks, seamen and traders, a primitive form of unarmed fighting had evolved.

Japan

At the turn of the 20th Century, the Russo-Japan War was in progress and Japan conscripted many Okinawans. An extremely alert Japanese Army doctor noticed the unusually well-proportioned and strong physiques of many Okinawan conscripts. Investigations revealed that such physiques were due to the practice of 'Te'. Japanese officials on Okinawa approved the inclusion of 'Te' in the physical education curriculum of Okinawan schools in 1902 because they could see the military advantages of such a system – that of conditioning future conscripts. Eventually 'Te' became known as Karate-Jutsu, the ideogram for which means 'Chinese hand art'. The then Japanese Emperor, Hirohito (29 April 1901 – 7 January 1989), while touring Okinawa in 1921 as the Crown Prince, witnessed a demonstration of Karate-Jutsu and was so favourably impressed that he included the event in his formal report to the Japanese government, which led to the Minister of Education inviting an Okinawan expert to Japan. Gichin Funakoshi was selected, not because the Okinawans felt he was the best exponent, but because he was a primary schoolteacher and his Japanese was very good. He also came from a family with a good background, which was essential if he was to gain any credibility.

Hoping to establish karate a lot earlier, Funakoshi had made an exploratory visit to the Japanese mainland in 1917 and given a demonstration of Karate-Jutsu to government

officials from the upper classes. Unfortunately, this meant that all spectators were descendants of Samurai. To them karate was seen to be nothing more than a set of exercises for street fighting without weapons, fit only for a plebeian class of people. Being of Samurai class, any form of combat which did not involve the use of a sword, was seen to be inferior. The Japanese were also very reluctant to accept any new form of combat which they had not developed themselves on mainland Japan.
Funakoshi's second visit to Japan was in 1922 and this time his display was open to the general public at the first sports festival held in Tokyo.

Funakoshi and Karate-Jutsu were an immediate success and before long, their great popularity among the young Japanese, especially university students, soon gave this art a larger following in Japan than in Okinawa.

Funakoshi quickly struck up a friendship with Jigoro Kano, the founder of modern day Judo. After many discussions, he adopted a style of uniform (gi) very similar to that worn by judo students. He also copied Kano's system of awarding black belts (Dan) to his senior students after a formal assessment.

This would prove invaluable, as it was one of the stipulations that the Dai Nippon Butoku Kai (Japanese controlling body for martial arts) required from prospective candidates. In 1931, karate was accepted into the association as long as the word karate was written in Japanese characters and not Chinese, a standard uniform was adopted, tournaments were held regularly and a black belt system was in force.

The rapid proliferation of Japanese Karate-Jutsu cannot however be accredited to the teachings of Gichin Funakoshi alone. Many skilled exponents have influenced the formation

Chris Thompson with two Washinkai seniors, Graham Smith (left) and Neville Smith

和心会

CHAPTER 1

of Japanese Karate-do and have shared in promoting its growth (see next chapter).

From the traditionalist's point of view, however, Funakoshi must be considered the Father of Japanese Karate-do insofar as he is responsible for making many important innovations to Karate-Jutsu that have brought this art closer to the Japanese and later, Western taste. In 1933 Funakoshi changed the concept of 'kara', which was originally written with a Chinese character meaning 'China hand', by substituting another character, also pronounced 'kara' but meaning 'void' or 'empty'. Therefore, Funakoshi's new Karate-Jutsu meant 'empty hand art'. Two years later, Funakoshi discarded the word 'jutsu' in favour of 'do' (the way of). Thus Karate-do was born in Japan and the literal meaning is 'empty hand way'.

Funakoshi established a central dojo (hall for training) in Tokyo in 1936 and, after much deliberation, gave it the name 'Shotokan'. The ideograms that read 'Shoto' are Funakoshi's pen name as a calligrapher; 'kan' means hall. This was to be the Honbu (headquarters) for his karate organisation.

World War II saw Karate-Jutsu and Karate-do become officially recognised as an invaluable part of the training process of the Japanese soldiers and sailors. The mass participation of Japan's young men resulted in the rapid development of new unarmed karate techniques, and even after the Japanese defeat, when most martial arts were prohibited as they were considered to foster militarism, karate systems continued to flourish. Fortunately, the Allied Powers believed these systems to be little more than physical education, similar to Chinese Boxing and did not ban them as they did with Kendo and Judo. The technical progress of karate-do in the 1950s and early 1960s quickly led to the formulation of a syllabus for each style. A

CHAPTER 1

national body was established by senior experts of several Ryu (schools) to ensure that high standards were maintained. This in turn led to the participation of great numbers of high school and university students entering karate-do competitions, making it a sport of popular appeal and national importance. Funakoshi had specific ideas in mind when he replaced the original character of 'kara' which meant 'China hand', to the modern meaning of 'empty'. The fact that Japanese karate-do does not involve the use of weapons, only parts of the body, gives literal meaning to the translation. But the obvious conflict of this change, with the fact that the Okinawan karate systems always included the use of specific weapons: Bo (6-foot staff), Nunchakus (rice flails), Tonfa (rice grinding handles), Sai (large metal-pronged forks), Kama (sickle) and Tekko (metal knuckle dusters) was one reason why Funakoshi's change of character angered the many traditionalists in Okinawa. Funakoshi clarified the apparent paradox and gained much support from his fellow Okinawans by declaring that the use of the ideogram 'kara' (empty) was based on the concept of 'unselfishness'. Thus, 'emptiness' suggested by the newly chosen character, referred to the state of rendering oneself 'empty' or 'egoless'. Funakoshi stressed he taught karate as an exercise for the mind and body to form personal character.

It was during the American Armed Forces' occupation of Japan after the War that Westerners gained their first sight of karate-do. Many US servicemen joined in classes of karate-do and, although there was Japanese resentment to foreigners in the classes, they had no option but to teach the Westerners, fearing that the rejection of these new students would result in closure of their classes and obvious loss of income. Once accepted by the Japanese, these American servicemen were taught the finer points of karate-do,

Chris Thompson with Shingo Ohgami

making it possible to pass their knowledge on when they were posted back to the United States. Many did set about teaching this strange art of karate-do upon their return, thus introducing Karate to the Americans in the early 1950s.

With Japanese and American trade rapidly expanding after the War, many senior Japanese karate-ka visited the United States. Today, every style of Japanese karate has a school somewhere in the USA and the practitioners number many thousands.

Europe

The interest for karate in Europe was sparked off by the Frenchman, Henri Plee. He is acknowledged to be the first man to bring a Japanese expert of karate-do to Europe in 1957. The first person credited with introducing karate-do to England was a Mr Vernon Bell who trained under Plee in Paris and later brought over from Japan a Shotokan stylist, Kanazawa-Sensei.

By the mid-1960s, the demand for karate was so great in Britain, that many Japanese karate-ka were invited to come over and teach on a permanent basis, as it was felt that the standard needed to be raised. Japanese practitioners of several styles were invited and as a result, we find many senior Japanese instructors resident in the UK, especially in the styles of Shotokan and Wado-Ryu. This early influence has created a nation of extremely adept karate-ka, regardless of style and is reflected in the fact that the Great Britain team has won the WUKO, now the WKF, world team championships on no less than five occasions. No other country in the world, including Japan, has managed this great feat.

CHAPTER 2

The major styles of karate-do

As mentioned in the previous chapter, Funakoshi was not the only Okinawan to teach karate on the mainland of Japan. Several of his fellow countrymen, also competent in karate-jutsu, left their homeland to teach this secret art. Some of these masters were able to settle in Japan whilst others quickly became homesick, but like Funakoshi, they eventually gave names to their systems of karate-jutsu.

SHOTOKAN – Founder Gichin Funakoshi (1868 – 1957)

Gichin Funakoshi, already acknowledged as the founder of modern day karate, was reluctant to call his style a 'ryu' (school). His teachings differed greatly by the 1930s from his contemporaries in Okinawa and also from the way he himself was taught. He had a profound effect upon all his students and placed much emphasis upon their mental awareness as well as their physical prowess. The Shotokan that we are familiar with today can be accredited more to Funakoshi's third son. He, like Hironori Ohtsuka, founder of Wado-Ryu, believed in applying the karate techniques in actual free-fighting. As with all the young men of that generation they wanted to test their skills on one another. By 1936 when Gichin Funakoshi established the Shotokan in Tokyo, he was 68 years of age. Even though he had a tremendous following, a lot of the burden was now placed on his son. The younger Funakoshi's style of karate was quite different to his father's. The older Funakoshi had always adopted high stances, whilst his son's were a lot lower. His son also used full leg extension techniques, such as Mawashigeri and Sokuto (Yoko-geri) with which he is given credit for introducing into karate. The kata of Shotokan are numerous and some even have derivations, which reflect the old Funakoshi's teachings. Today, Shotokan is the largest style of karate-do practiced worldwide.

GOJU-RYU – Founder Chojun Miyagi (1888 – 1953)

Goju-Ryu, meaning hard/soft school, was founded by the Okinawan Chojun Miyagi, one of the few students of the great Kannryo Higoanna, a Naha-te karate instructor. Miyagi studied with him until his death in 1915 and then travelled to China to continue his studies of various forms of Wushu. Upon his return to Okinawa, he merged his Wushu teachings (soft) with his Naha-te (hard). Like other Okinawans who were extremely competent, Miyagi was asked to teach his Goju-Ryu in Japan. He travelled to Kyoto and other cities but found himself extremely homesick. Gogen Yamaguchi was the last disciple of Miyagi before he returned to Okinawa. Yamaguchi created a typical Japanese style of Goju-Ryu with lots of emphasis on internal strength. There are presently two Goju schools, the Okinawan and Japanese. Both are well represented internationally.

SHITO-RYU – Founder Kenwa Mabuni (1889 – 1952)

Kenwa Mabuni, an Okinawan like Funakoshi, had as his instructor Kannryo Higoanna, the instructor of Chojun Miyagi – founder of Goju-Ryu and Anko Itosu – one of Funakoshi's instructors. This gave Mabuni a chance to practise Naha kata as well as Shuri and Tomari kata. Being a close friend of Chojun Miyagi's, he also visited China with him to study the Chinese Wushu forms. With such an amassed amount of knowledge, Mabuni created a style based on over 60 kata (forms) and called it Hanko-Ryu. He eventually changed the name to Shito-Ryu which was an amalgamation of the two instructors' names: Itosu and Higoanna. Like Funakoshi, he travelled to Japan in the late 1920s and settled in Osaka, where he taught his Shito-Ryu. It is a very popular style in Japan, more so in the western part of the country and is now gaining popularity in the Western world.

CHAPTER 2

KYOKUSHINKAI – Founder Matsutatsu Oyama (1923 – 1994)

Mas. Oyama, a Korean born naturalised Japanese, developed Kyokushinkai (school of ultimate truth) a style which was as close to combat as one could get. His concept of one punch, one kick technique, to stop an opponent is the foundation of the style. He was greatly influenced by both Funakoshi and Gogen Yamaguchi of Goju-Kai, but found neither conveyed the true combative spirit. After a self-imposed, solitary period, he re-emerged to demonstrate his own style of karate, by fighting bulls barehanded, successfully killing three each with a single blow. This gave Oyama immediate popularity, even having a cartoon strip in a national magazine. His style was the fastest growing of all the karate styles throughout the world. Its popularity was due to its dynamic actions and it appealed to spectators in the same way as the gladiators in the coliseums of ancient Rome. Oyama's knockdown tournaments, which rely on the opponent being knocked down in order to determine the winner, had a massive appeal to the young. It is a style which proudly boasts to be extremely hard and unrelenting in its training. The style continues to grow since the death of Oyama in 1994.

CHAPTER 3

 **CHAPTER 3**

WADO-RYU – Founder Hironori Ohtsuka 1892 – 1982

The reason I have devoted a whole chapter and gone into greater detail on the origins of Wado-Ryu karate, is that the students of the style at whom this book is aimed, will find its history, as well as that of its founder, very interesting.

The founder of Wado-Ryu, Hironori Ohtsuka, was born on the 1st June 1892 in Shimodate City, Ibaraki Prefecture, Japan and by the time he was 6 years of age, had already started training in Ju-Jitsu, studying under his maternal Grand-Uncle. Upon entering middle school at the age of 13, he started to study Shindo Yoshin-Ryu Ju-Jitsu under Tatsusabaro Nakayama. These studies continued with Nakayama throughout his education at Waseda University, resulting in Ohtsuka being awarded his menkyo (licence) level of proficiency in Shindo Yoshin-Ryu by Nakayama in 1921.

In 1922 Ohtsuka heard of the karate demonstration given by Gichin Funakoshi in Tokyo and was determined to meet him. Throughout his studies of Ju-Jitsu, Ohtsuka always sought out other styles of Ju-Jitsu trying to visit as many different dojo as possible. With the advent of a completely new weaponless martial art, Ohtsuka could not contain his excitement. He met Funakoshi at his residence, the 'Meisei Juku', the house for Okinawan students, in the same year. They talked for several hours discussing their own interpretations of the martial arts and by the end of that evening.

Funakoshi agreed to accept Ohtsuka as a student of his karate jutsu. Ohtsuka started training with Funakoshi immediately. And because of his enthusiasm and martial arts background, quickly grasped the physical techniques that he was being taught. In just over a year he had studied and knew the movements of every kata that Funakoshi had taught him. Kata was the only aspect of karate being taught by Funakoshi at the time. Throughout this period, Ohtsuka did not cease his training in Ju-Jitsu and began to incorporate this into his karate jutsu. He developed Yakusoku kumite (pre-arranged sparring) and when he showed these techniques with his partner to Funakoshi, they were warmly greeted.

In April 1924, Ohtsuka aged 31, along with six others, was graded to Shodan level by Funakoshi – thus becoming one of the first Japanese to receive a black belt in karate. The following month both Funakoshi and Ohtsuka gave the first public display of these new Yakusoku kumite techniques.

The continued devotion to both Ju-Jitsu and karate jutsu led to Ohtsuka becoming a Shihan (Chief Instructor) in Shindo Yoshin-Ryu and Funakoshi's assistant instructor He also began to train with other famous martial artists, such as Kenwa Mabuni (founder of Shito-Ryu) and Choki Motobu. As a proficient karate instructor, he began teaching at Tokyo University and his methods began to conflict with Funakoshi's teachings. Ohtsuka's brand of karate, incorporating his Ju-Jitsu techniques, enabled his students to practice free sparring. This was not to Funakoshi's liking, as his concepts of karate differed greatly from Ohtsuka's. Funakoshi felt that actual fighting (Jissen) was far too dangerous and would immediately result in the death of one of the participants. On the other hand, Ohtsuka believed with specific guidelines and rules that students could use techniques in a free fighting form without severe injury.

The departure by Ohtsuka from Funakoshi was inevitable. Over a period of several years, Ohtsuka integrated all his Ju-Jitsu knowledge into his karate jutsu creating many aspects unique to his style of karate. He created kihon kumite as well as Yakusoku Kumite. He taught a more upright stance giving greater mobility.

Emphasis was placed on Tai-sabaki (hip evasion) and immediate counter techniques rather than pure strength to intercept an attack. He introduced throws and locks into the pair techniques. The use of hip twist whilst driving out a punch, yet keeping the arm relaxed, was developed by Ohtsuka, as well as the snapping back action on all techniques. He reduced the amount of kata in his repertoire, all learnt from Funakoshi, and reverted to their original names, either Chinese or Okinawan. Example: the Heians of Shotokan were given their original name of Pinans as named by their Okinawan creator, Anko Itosu (1830 – 1915), who also taught Funakoshi.

Above all, the introduction of Ji-yu kumite (free sparring) as standard practice in all his classes, singled out Ohtsuka's style of karate. He even held a rudimentary karate competition in 1929.

Eventually, Ohtsuka named the style Wado-Ryu (way of peace school) (see Chapter 10) and gained the seal of approval very quickly from the Dai Nippon Butoku Kai who awarded him the title 'Renshi' in 1938.

After the War there were very few qualified karate instructors prepared to devote themselves to the development of karate, Ohtsuka was one. Wado-Ryu's rapid growth was not only due to Ohtsuka's innovative karate technique, but also his philosophy on karate.

He firmly believed that through 'Shugyo' (austere training) one could gain physical as well as spiritual discipline. Ohtsuka was a very moral man and always showed great concern for his students.

Many of them, who are now senior instructors of Wado-Ryu, called him a 'gentle man' and treated him as a father figure.

One of the greatest rewards of his career was to be decorated in 1966, at the age of 74, by Emperor Hirohito with the

CHAPTER 3

Shiju Hoosho Medal for his distinguished service to karate-do. He was the only karate-ka to have such an award bestowed on him and indicated the extent to which karate had been accepted by the government in Japan.

Wado-Ryu's early grounding in the competition field has led to many successes for the organisation. Because speed is a major factor in the execution of technique and body positioning, Wado-Ryu has created many world champions.

Sadly, Ohtsuka died at the beginning of 1982, a few months short of his 90th birthday. Up to then, he had been the oldest active karate-ka. Ohtsuka abdicated his position as headmaster of the worldwide Wado-ryu organisation two months before his death and nominated his son, Jiro Ohtsuka, as his successor. Unfortunately, this was not well accepted by many of the senior instructors and a large rift was created. Let us hope that a reconciliation comes about.

Today, there are over 100 various systems of karate-do in Japan. The vast majority can trace their origins back to one of the five styles that I have written about. In the United Kingdom all the major Japanese and Okinawan styles of karate-do are represented and those styles that have originated on these shores can easily be linked to one of the five major Ryu.

CHAPTER 4

 **CHAPTER 4**

Short History of Christopher Thompson and Washinkai Karate-Do Renmei

I began to learn karate in June 1969, just before Man had landed on the moon and the Beatles were still at the height of their popularity. We were about to go into the decade of the 1970s and it was a time of euphoria. The Japanese dominated karate in the UK and were revered. I remember getting quite nervous entering the dojo when a new visiting Japanese Sensei was present.

At 11 years of age I suffered a severe eye injury which prevented participation in physical sports for several years. Once the doctors had cleared me for physical activities I decided I wanted to do a sport that was different. I chose karate as it was relatively new and unknown. For two years, I tried learning karate from several instructors, but felt I was getting nowhere. Finally, I enrolled at the 'Judokan' in Hammersmith, London and remember having to be proposed and seconded for membership by Percy Sekine (1920 – 2010) as I was under 18 years of age. The style I was learning was Wado-ryu karate. This was not by choice, but, like most students, one does not realise until some months into karate that you are doing a specific style. It's just karate.

My first Wado-ryu instructor was Bob Wignall, who died in June 2005. Before long, I was training with the Chief Instructor of Wado Ryu in the UK, Tatsuo Suzuki 8th Dan (1928 – 2011), who then taught at King's Cross, London. I was amazed how such a small, elderly man could move with such speed and generate so much power. He, together with many of his Japanese teachers, inspired me and made me train more diligently, albeit parrot fashion as in-depth explanation of techniques was not their way.

I quickly gained Shodan (first black belt) and being young, started to explore other styles of karate believing that they were inferior. Thus was the state of my mind at the time. I had a rude awakening with Shotokan and Kyokushinkai stylists and realised that their karate was good.

Bruce Lee exploded on to the scene in the early 1970s and with two small clubs, I soon found my membership quadrupled overnight. I still maintain that even though Bruce Lee had his critics, he brought the martial arts to the forefront of media attention and made Kung Fu and Karate household names.

In 1973 the Wado-Ryu organisation I belonged to, whose senior instructors were all Japanese, split into two major factions. This was a major blow to me. I had trained seriously since witnessing these Japanese experts execute flawless technique. I had become quite friendly with two Japanese Sensei (teacher) and now both were in separate camps. My dilemma was loyalty. I tried to hedge my bets by training with both organisations, but found this to be too difficult as both had separate syllabuses and I was constantly being corrected by each instructor. Finally, I decided to abandon one for the other, which gave me some harmony for a short period.

I can never criticise the period I spent learning Wado-Ryu with the Japanese instructors here in England, nor the style itself. My learning curve was a quick one and I hold many pleasant memories of both Mr Naomich Kitamura and Mr Tadayuki Maeda, who was a Japanese national champion.

The knowledge they passed on to me was priceless. I had many interesting experiences. For example, during this period, Mr Hironori Ohtsuka (1892 – 1982) the Founder of Wado-Ryu, visited the dojo whilst I was teaching. He stayed and watched together

CHAPTER 4

with other visiting dignitaries until the end of the class. His comments to me afterwards, through an interpreter, were very rewarding and I shall never forget them.

In early 1977, for many reasons, I severed all my connections with the Wado-Ryu organisation, led by the Japanese here in the UK, I was totally dissatisfied and disillusioned.

I now went searching for a new home, which involved training with various senior instructors of different schools of karate. This period was invaluable as it broadened my horizons, giving me an insight into the different approach that other instructors had in teaching karate. I made many good friends. For over a year I continued with this programme whilst running several clubs. I admired many aspects of all the karate schools I trained with, but I felt that none could offer exactly what I was looking for. Unbeknown to me at the time I was following the steps of Shu-ha-ri.

With five clubs spread over London we collectively called ourselves Wa-Shin-Kai. This was not a new style, but a name to identify with: Wa – for harmony, as my roots were with Wado-Ryu; Shin – for heart, mind and spirit as one, also truth; Kai – for group.

One particular student, Colin Inwood, who started as a beginner with me in 1975, helped create a specific growth programme for Washinkai. We both felt high standards had to be maintained at all levels if we were going to survive as an independent group and that there was no contradiction in teaching methods or technique.

Washinkai also had the benefits of two Japanese instructors who had come to the clubs and stayed for long periods; Hironori Goda, a Goju stylist, Takao Yamamoto, a Shito-ryu stylist. Over a period of several years a grading syllabus was formulated, to take the student from beginner to Shodan level (black belt). Both these Japanese men, upon their return to Japan, continued with the Washinkai teaching programme. Our growth was not rapid as we had specifically adhered to the policy of growth from within. By the time we had grown to 12 clubs, Washinkai was evolving into a Wado-Ryu based style, rather than just a collective name as everything was slightly different from other styles of karate.

Washinkai Karate Do Renmei now has many clubs in England as well as Japan, Spain, Ireland and Norway. Washinkai were founder members of the English Karate Governing Body (EKGB), which was founded in 1991, and at the time was the only karate governing body recognised by Sport England. I was the Technical Chairman for the EKGB upon its demise in 2005.

I presently hold the grade of 8th Dan, recognised by the World Karate Federation (WKF) and also hold the office of Director of the English Karate Federation.

left to right - Chris Thompson with Norwegian Chief Instructor Geir Støre, and with Yoshinobu Ohta of the Japan Karate Association.

和心会　　CHAPTER 4

CHAPTER 5

Calisthenics
(Warming up and stretching exercises)

It is very important that warming up and stretching exercises are carried out before commencing your karate training. They should be done systematically and regularly with many repetitions. Some need to be done slowly and deliberately. The body temperature should be raised through exercising and stretching to prevent any injury occurring.

Deep stretching, especially for the legs, is necessary to improve flexibility and speed. These must be carried out carefully and not taken to extremes. Your body will let you know when to stop.

Warming down exercises

These are just as important after a training session to bring your body temperature back to normal and to relax your muscles and respiratory system.

1. Palms pressed together, fingers pointing outwards, push hands firmly together bringing both hands into the chest. Hold for 5 seconds and repeat. This exercise stretches the tendons in the wrist.

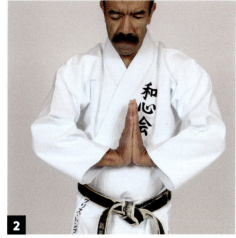

2. Fingers pointing upwards, hold for 5 seconds and repeat.

3
Fingers pointing downwards, hold for 5 seconds and repeat.

4
Place right hand on the back of the left and push left hand back on itself. Immediately change to exercise right wrist.

5
Place right hand underneath fingertips of left hand and push left hand backwards. Immediately change to exercise right wrist.

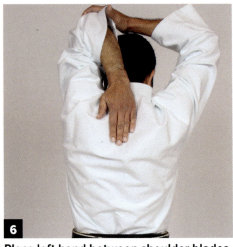

6
Place left hand between shoulder blades using other hand gently push elbow down. Hold for 15 seconds, but do not push too severely. The triceps and shoulders are stretched. Repeat with the other arm.

CHAPTER 5 Calisthenics

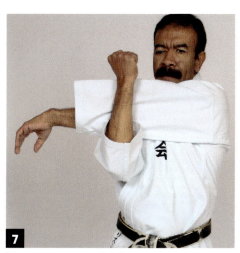

7 Place arm across body, and use the other arm behind the elbow and pull backwards towards you. Repeat on the other side.

8 Placing hands on hips, legs comfortably astride, lean to the right. Do not lean forwards or backwards. Hold for 15 seconds. Repeat, leaning to the left.

9 Keeping hands on hips, legs comfortably astride, lean forward from the hip, keeping spine straight. Hold for 15 seconds.

10 Repeat this time leaning backwards. Hold for 15 seconds.

Place leg at 45 degrees from the body, hands behind your back and lean over the leg, repeat on opposite side.

Stretching the hamstring. Lean towards right leg slowly, ensuring the toes are raised upwards and hold position for 15 seconds. Repeat on other leg

Repeat exercise but this time place instep down on the floor. Repeat on other leg.

Stretch out both legs supporting bodyweight with hand, maintaining position walk forwards until knees touch the floor, raise hold and hold for 30 seconds.

CHAPTER 5 — Calisthenics

15 Pull soles of feet together and hold on to toes, pulling yourself forward stretching the groin. A partner can assist by pushing the knees gently down. Hold for 20-30 seconds.

16 Place left leg in front of partner's outstretched left leg and push their body towards the outstretched right leg, keeping the back supported. Hold for 30 seconds and repeat on other side.

17 With legs fully stretched a partner can assist by pushing the body forward gently, supporting the spine with both hands at all times. This should be done slowly, hold for 30 seconds.

18 Placing the straight left leg on partner's right shoulder, the hamstring is stretched, to fully stretch lean forward placing head against knee. Hold for 30 seconds and repeat on other side.

CHAPTER 6

CHAPTER 6 — Kihon

Kihon

The basic techniques of karate: punching, kicking and blocking, are called Kihon. It is essential before one can advance in karate that the fundamentals are grasped. This is why kihon training is so necessary. Unfortunately, because it is so repetitive and the techniques after a while seem so simple, many students become disillusioned and leave karate. This is a shame, as many potentially good karate-ka quit at an early stage. The Japanese adopt a different attitude to kihon training. They realised that a house can only be built on a solid foundation. A period of at least 30 minutes should be devoted to kihon training in any session.

It is during this sort of rigorous training that strong technique is developed, especially on the body's weaker side. Up to 500 repetitions of a single technique is not uncommon and can only be beneficial. The main aid for the solitary practice of kihon is a mirror where incorrect technique can be improved.

Correct Kokyu (breathing) is essential when carrying out any manoeuvre in karate and this can be perfected through your kihon training. Always remember to expel the air in the body when exerting oneself, especially through Kiai. Never carry out strenuous technique without taking good quantities of air.

Through constant kihon training all the other aspects of your karate will improve.

Type of Hand

1

Ippon Nukite: one finger spear hand. This would be used primarily to attack an eye.

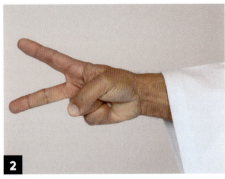

2

Nihon Nukite: two finger spear hand. Again primarily used for eye attacks.

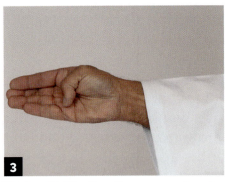

3

Yonhon Nukite: four finger spear hand. Attacks to the eye and throat especially, but it can also be used to the stomach.

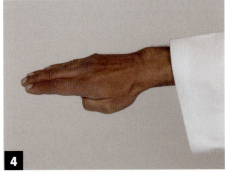

4

Haito: ridge hand. The thumb should be tucked underneath. This technique should be used to attack the face, neck stomach or groin,

5

Ippon Ken: one knuckle fist. Ideal for attacking the ribs or face.

6

Shuto-Uchi: knife hand, Targets are limitless as the strike is extremely strong.

CHAPTER 6 — Kihon

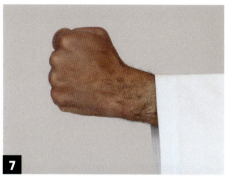

7 Uraken: back fist. The striking area should be the back of the two first knuckles. Popular target is the face, but is often used to the stomach.

8 Teisho: palm heel. This is used to strike underneath the chin or, if inverted the solar plexus or groin.

10 Kakuto-Uchi: wrist strike. Use to the neck only.

9 Tettsui-Uchi: bottom fist, Like shuto, the target area is limitless.

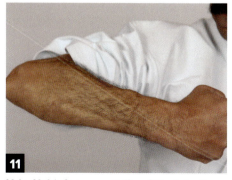

11 Ude-Uchi: forearm strike. Attack to the ribs or face.

12 Empi-Uchi: elbow strike. Limitless striking areas.

Type of Foot

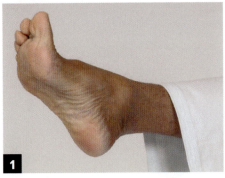

1

Josokutei: ball of foot. The striking area of Maegeri (front kick). Targets are limitless.

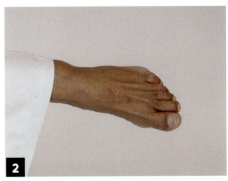

2

Ashikubi: front of foot: Used with Mawashigeri (roundhouse kick). Targets are limitless

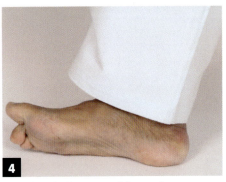

4

Fumikomi: close up of foot edge.

5

Hiza-Geri: Knee strike. Target areas, groin, stomach and face.

7

Mukozune-Geri: shin kick, striking area - knee joint, thigh, ribs and head

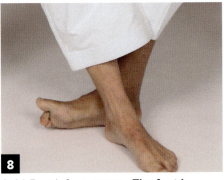

8

Ashi-Barai: foot sweep. The foot is positioned in the same way as Sokuto Fumikomi. Sweeping must be made with the sole of the foot.

CHAPTER 6 — Kihon

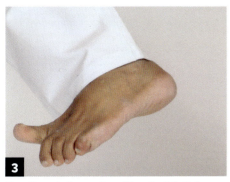

3 Fumikomi: foot edge. Used with Sokuto (side kick). Targets - knees, stomach, throat.

6 Kakato-Geri: heel kick. Used extensively with axe kick. Striking areas are limitless.

Making a Correct Fist

F6

F1 Hand open.

F2 Pull fingers in

F3 Bring thumb over top

F4 Clench fist with thumb resting on first and second finger, compressing all the air out of fist.

F5 Side view of correct fist with back of wrist completely flat.

Stances

1

Heisoku-Dachi: (formal attention stance) big toes and heels touching, hands by your side, back straight, looking directly in front.

2

Musubi-Dachi: (informal attention stance). As Heisoku-Dachi, but heels touching only.

3

Hachiji-Dachi: open leg stance. The position adopted in Yoi (ready stance).

4

Shizentai-Dachi: natural stance. Used with Tobikomizuki and Nagashizuki.

5

Sanchin-Dachi: Hour-glass stance. Used primarily in kata.

6

Kiba-Dachi: horse-riding stance. Again, used primarily in kata.

CHAPTER 6   Kihon

7
Shiko-Dachi: straddle stance. Knees and toes pointing outwards. Used in kata.

8
Neko-ashi-Dachi: cat stance. 60% of weight on back foot, 40 % on ball of front foot. Kata stance.

9
Gyaku-neko-ashi-Dachi: reverse of Neko-ashi-Dachi. Again, used in kata.

10
Kokutsu-Dachi: back stance. 70% of weight on back foot, 30% on front. Primarily used in kata.

11
Sagi-ashi-Dachi: crane stance. All weight on one leg. Kata stance.

Rei (Bowing)

At the beginning of each class, formal bows are undertaken, The commands are often accompanied by a Dojo-kun. The instructor or senior student will call the command 'Seiza', to adopt the bow position. Adopt Musubi-Dachi **1**, Place right knee on floor directly in front **2**, Bend both knees, going down with the right knee pointing directly in front, hands holding top of the Zubon (gi bottoms) up, bring left knee up parallel to right knee placing it on the floor **3** and sit down on insteps resting both hands on top of thighs. Back should be kept straight, looking directly in front **4**.

At this point the Dojo-kun is chanted by either students, Instructor, or both and then the Instructor will command 'Sensei Ni Rei' bow to the Instructor. All students as well as the Instructor will bow. Lean forward, bringing the hands forward in a circular motion, until finger tips touch **5**, Keep looking up and return to position **4**. The second command will be 'Otagai Ni Rei' - bow to everybody. All students will bow but not the Instructor. Finally the command will be 'Kiritsu' - stand to attention. Raise left knee **6**, placing weight onto sole of left foot and at the same time go on to the ball of the right foot. Retract left leg back into Musubi-Dachi **1**.

Zenkutsu-Dachi (Junzuki stance)

CHAPTER 6   **Kihon**

1

Musubi-Dachi

The Instructor will give the command 'Hidari Gamae-Junzuki' (left Junzuki stance)

2

Adopt Yoi stance, stepping out with left leg underneath left shoulder, fist clenched, right leg underneath right shoulder, fist clenched.

3

Pull both hands back onto hip slide left leg forward.

4

Left foot should be placed down bending the left knee so that the lower leg is at right angles to the floor. The right leg is locked straight.

5

Punch out with the left fist, keeping elbow tucked in. On completion of the punch rotate the fist to that the back of the hand faces upwards.

Whilst moving forward practising Junzuki, remember not to raise your height whilst stepping forward, and to keep both arms perfectly still until the front foot touches the floor. Then punch as quickly as possible, retracting the non punching hand back on to the hip, with equal speed. The weight is equally distributed on both legs.

Turning from Junzuki

1

Rear view of right Junzuki punch, the Instructor will give the command 'Mawatte Jodan Uke' when he wants you to turn 180 degrees.

2

Bring left leg across, stretching outwards approximately twice the width of your own shoulders, before stopping. Pivot round on the balls of the feet, keeping upper body perfectly still.

3

Start crossing the arms, with the left going under the right.

4

The right arm is now completely across the body with the left arm underneath the right arm.

5

Continue to sweep the left arm across the face to prevent an attack performing Jodan Soto-Uke.

6

Alternatively raise the left arm above the face, performing Jodan-Uke. The arm must be at an angle above the head and the right arm retracted back onto the right hip.

CHAPTER 6　　Kihon

1 Still in left Junzuki stance the Instructor will give the command 'Sono Ba De Ippon Toru'.

2 Begin to punch out with the right arm, retracting the left arm. The left leg is also retracted.

3 The left leg begins to go out slightly as the punch nears completion.

Changing from Junzuki-Dachi to Gyakuzuki-Dachi

The whole action is carried out at speed.

Again, like Junzuki, whilst practising Gyakuzuki on the move. The height should not be raised with each step forward. It is also important to twist the front foot out before stepping in and out in a diagonal motion with the back leg. Full hip twist and a substantial amount of shoulder twist is incorporated in the punch, yet the spine must be kept perfectly straight and look directly in front.

4 The transition is made with a full extension right punch and the stance shortened slightly.

Turning from Gyakuzuki-Dachi

1 Rear view of left Gyakuzuki. The Instructor will give the command 'Mawatte Gedan-Barai'.

2 Side view.

3 Bring left leg across, stretching outwards approximately twice the width of your own shoulders.

4 Place left punching arm across the chest with bottom of the fist pressing into the upper chest.

5 As you pivot round 180 degrees, begin to bring left arm downwards.

6 Your stance locks into Junzuki as the arm comes further down.

7 Gedan-Barai. Lock your left arm parallel to your left thigh as you complete the block against a kick.

The Tsuki-Waza (punching technique) shown are fundamental techniques of Wado-Ryu karate. In addition, all four manoeuvres can be practised with kicks. These will be introduced at a later stage as the students techniques improve. The four additional techniques are called: Kette Junzuki, Kette Gyakuzuki, Kette Junzuki No Tsukkomi, Kette Gyakuzuki No Tsukkomi. All have Chudan aimed Maegeris (see page 56) incorporated into the technique.

CHAPTER 6 — Kihon

Junzuki No Tsukkomi Dachi

J1 — Front view of left Junzuki No Tsukkomi.

J2 — Side view

This punch is directed to the face with the stance extremely narrow and the bodyweight distributed with 60% over the front leg. For an opponent, the target area offered is very limited. Stepping forward is carried out in the same manner as Junzuki, except that the stance is narrower. Turning is done to either the command 'Mawatte Jodan Uke' or 'Mawatte Soto Uke' and is done in exactly the same manner as the Junzuki block.

Gyakuzuki No Tsukkomi Dachi

G1 — Front view of right Gyakuzuki No Tsukkomi.

G2 — Side view.

Like Gyakuzuki, the technique is a reverse punch (i.e. reverse limbs). The difference being the punch is directed to the groin area with the stance being wider and not so deep. The body leans forward yet the back is kept straight. Practising the technique moving forward, it is important not to yo-yo up and down, yet maintain the same height. Obviously, because the stance is so wide and hardly any distance gained stepping forward, it will take you twice as many steps to cover the same distance. Turning is carried out in exactly the same way as 'Mawatte Gedan Barai' on Gyakuzuki, except one needs to stretch out considerably more with the back leg to end up a correct Zenkutsu Dachi.

Keri-Waza

Kicking techniques separates Karate from Boxing. The multiple use of kicks makes Karate a much more versatile combative art. The practice of Keri-Waza is more functional than Tsuki-waza as the stances and kicks are put into practice in exactly the same way as they would be executed in a real fight situation.

This technique is practised up and down the Dojo, do not bob up and down whilst moving forward, keep your body at a 45 degree angle at all times.

The Instructor will give the command 'Hidari Hanmi Gamae' (left fighting stance).

Maegeri (front kick)

3a

1
Both knees are bent and the guard is kept high.

2
Raise the knee so the thigh is parallel to the floor.

3
Thrust the right leg forward striking with the ball of the foot and pushing the hip into the kick, snap the leg back.

Mawashigeri (roundhouse kick)

CHAPTER 6   **Kihon**

1
From left fighting stance raise right knee.

2
Pivot on the supporting leg, twisting the hip and turning the supporting foot around to 120 degrees minimum.

3
Extend right leg fully, ensuring you have rotated the hips through 180 degrees. Strike with Ashikubi (instep). Snap leg back before placing down into right stance.

3a
Side view

Mawashigeri is an extremely powerful kick and the ball of the foot can also be used to strike with. Practitioners can effectively strike any part of the body with this technique. Like Maegeri, ensure you do not raise your height whilst moving forward and get all your bodyweight behind the kick.

Surikomi Maegeri

1

Migi Hanmi Gamae (right fighting stance).

2

Keeping the same height, step up with the left leg, upon completing the step gain at least a metre.

3

Raise the knee.

4

Kick as normal Maegeri, snapping back the leg after completion.

This technique enables you to kick an opponent who is either out of distance or is rushing into you. With your bodyweight moving forward the technique generates more power. Surikomi (step forward) can be an addition to any kicking technique.

Sokuto Fumikomi (side kick)

CHAPTER 6 — **Kihon**

1

Hidari Hanmi Gamae (left fighting stance)

2

Raise right knee

3

Pivot body round on the supporting leg, covering the body with the kicking leg.

This technique is extremely powerful. It is stamping kick when delivered to the knee and not a thrusting motion. It is important that the back is kept straight upon execution so the energy travels straight down the body to the edge of the foot.

4

Thrust or stamp downwards to the knee, ensuring that the toes are pulled backwards and the body is kept straight.

5

Side kick (side view)

Ushiro-Geri (back kick)

1 Starting in Hidari Hanmi Gamae.

2 Bring left leg across body approximately one foot, no more.

3 Pivot on the balls of your feet, twisting your hips and upper body.

Like Sokuto this technique is very powerful. However it must be executed extremely fast as your back is momentarily turned to your opponent. Once mastered it can have devastating results.

4 With your back completely turned to your opponent, transfer the weight onto your left leg and raise knee (right) high into chest.

5 Begin to lean forward and extend your right leg. Kick out powerfully with your leg, keeping your body parallel to the floor.

6 It is important that your back is kept straight with your kicking leg, snap the leg back and turn very quickly after the execution of the technique. The whole manoeuvre is carried out in a split second.

Ura-Mawashi-Geri (hook kick)

CHAPTER 6 **Kihon**

1

Hidari Hanmi Gamae

2

Raise the right knee bringing it across the body

3

As the leg is extended, the hips begin to twist around and the supporting foot twists a minimum of 120 degrees away from you..

4

The leg is extended and the striking area is either the heel or the sole of the foot.

This technique is comparatively modern. It is a roundhouse kick in reverse and, if mastered, along with Mawashigeri, increases the versatility of the karateka's repertoire.

Turning from a fighting stance

1 Migi Hanmi Gamae.

2 Stretch across behind you with the back leg.

3 Begin to pivot round, as the body turns 180 degrees, the left hand comes off the hip and rises, the right hand begins to come down on to the hip.

4 On completion, the hands have changed position and you are now facing your opponent.

All the keri-waza so far has been practised up and down the dojo and when the instructor wants you to turn 180 degrees, he will give the command 'Mawatte'.

The technique of turning is a simple one and must be completed quickly. Quite often, in many schools of Wado-Ryu, a strong Kiai is given at this point.

Tsuki-Waza
Tobikomizuki (front snap punch)

CHAPTER 6 — **Kihon**

1 Hidari Shizentai.

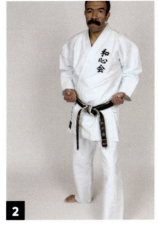

2 Slide the left leg forward pulling both hands back onto the hip.

3 As the leg moves forward, the hands are raised.

This manoeuvre is executed from a Shizentai (natural) stance and is an exercise in explosive attacking from a totally relaxed stance.

4 The stance adopted is Junzuki No Tsukkomi Dachi and the left fist punches to the face. The right fist comes up to protect the chest.

5 Snap the punching fist back, keep looking forward (Kime) and pull the back leg up halfway.

6 Retract the leg back into Shizentai Dachi, dropping both arms down.

Nagashizuki (front snap punch incorporating Taisabaki)

1 Hidari Shizentai.

2 Slide the left leg forward pulling both hands up.

3 Begin to pivot on the front leg pulling the straight right leg to the left.

Both Tobikomizuki and Nagashizuki are executed at full speed with maximum power. Throughout the execution, Kime should be demonstrated. Upon completion of the punch, in both techniques, there should be a moment's delay, zanshin, before retracting back into the natural stance.

4 Stop the taisabaki (hip shift) after you have travelled approximately two feet, no more and punch. This manoeuvre is executed simultaneously.

5 Snap the punching fist back.

6 Bring the right leg across and forward diagonally. Retract the front leg back into Shizentai Dachi, dropping both arms down, as in **1**.

Advanced Keri-Waza
Mikazuki-Geri Uchi (inner crescent kick)

CHAPTER 6 Kihon

I1 Starting in Hidari Hanmi Gamae raise the right knee, keeping it slightly to the right of the body.

I2 Extend the leg, angling the foot to a Fumikomi position.

I3 Swing the leg inwards across the body, striking with the sole or the inside of the foot. Finish by landing in Migi Hanmi Gamae.

Mikazuki-Geri Soto (outer crescent kick)

01 Starting in Hidari Hanmi Gamae, raise the right knee across the body.

02 Extend the leg, angling the foot to a Fumikomi position, swinging the leg across the body.

03 Strike with the outside of the foot, snap the leg back before placing it down in to Migi Hanmi Gamae.

Ushiro-Mawashi-Geri (back roundhouse kick)

1

From Hidari Hanmi Gamae bring left leg across the body as though about execute Ushiro-geri.

2

Pivot on the ball of the left foot and raise the right leg, keeping it fairly straight.

3

With a spinning momentum bring the right leg round. It is being elevated like a helicopter blade.

This technique is extremely powerful. It must be practised regularly before it can be incorporated in a karateka's repertoire. For without control, this is a dangerous technique.

4

Continue to spin on the left supporting leg, twisting the foot right round.

5

Strike either with the heel or the sole of the foot to the given target.

6

Snap the kicking leg back and land in Migi Hanmi Gamae.

Nidangeri (jumping double kick)

CHAPTER 6   **Kihon**

1 Migi Hanmi Gamae

2 Raise the left knee high as though about to step into the air.

3 As you ascend bring your right knee up.

4 Whilst still ascending, kick out with the right leg to head height.

This old technique, like many Tobi (jumping) kicks, was designed to knock riders off their horses.

As soon as the technique has been delivered, snap the kicking leg back and land back into Migi Hanmi Gamae. Do not jar your spine by landing on the soles of your feet. Try to land softly on the balls of your feet.

CHAPTER 7

CHAPTER 7 — Kata

Kata
The Five Pinans

The five Pinans (peaceful mind) kata covered in this chapter, were originated by Anko Itosu, one of Gichin Funakoshi's teachers, to facilitate the spreading of karate-jutsu amongst the schoolchildren of Okinawa.

Karate was introduced into the school curriculum in 1902 and Itosu felt that the forms Kushanku and Nai-hanchi were too difficult for the youngsters to grasp. Also, as a programme for karate was being created for such a large number of children, the Pinans helped towards giving the teaching a structure.

The syllabuses of modern day Wado-Ryu karate have the same principle, as the Pinans are usually included in the first few kyu grades prior to brown belt (3rd kyu) where the Kushanku kata is performed. Many aspects of Kushanku are obviously visible in the Pinans.

Like Yakusoku Kumite techniques, Kata should initially be practised slowly, progressively getting faster, and stronger. Kime and Zanshin (awareness) should be apparent at all times. The regular practice of kata is essential and instructors must teach the Bunkai (practical application) of each move for the student to thoroughly understand each kata.

As I stated in the Preface, some moves may differ from the way you have been taught the Pinans. I have tried to show the kata as close to their original format when created by Itosu. This has come about through many discussions and training sessions with senior instructors of various Ryu in the UK, America and Japan. The structure of all the Pinans should be the same and you will be able to follow any interpretations quite easily.

Finally, these basic kata which seem to have simple techniques often disguise very high level and hidden techniques. When practising the bunkai of these kata, one can see how clever Itosu was as the most simple block can be translated into a powerful blow.

Pinan Nidan (Ipponme Kata)

Of the five Pinan Katas, Pinan Nidan is by far the easiest to perform. There are fewer moves in this kata than in the others and each move is comparatively simple. In my organisation, the kata is referred to as Ipponme Kata to avoid confusion as it is always taught prior to the other Pinan Kata. Pinan Nidan means Pinan Number 2.

The moves may differ in this format from the Pinan Nidan you are taught, but closely follow Itosu's original moves. The variation practised by most Wado-Ryu students are shown in the Appendix at the end of the book.

All the movements in Pinan Nidan kata are performed at full speed and full power.

1
Yoi position.

2
Step to the left with the left leg, raising left arm across the chest.

3
Step down into Hidari Zenkutsu Dachi blocking down left Gedan Barai.

CHAPTER 7 — Ipponme

4 Step forward punching Migi Junzuki

5 Step across with the left leg, crossing both arms in front of the chest.

6 Turn 180° into Hidari Zenkutsu and perform left Gedan Barai.

7 Step forward punching Migi Junzuki.

8 Step forward again punching Hidari Junzuki.

9 Step to the left with the left leg at 90° bringing the left arm across the chest.

10 Step down into Hidari Zenkutsu Dachi blocking left Gedan Barai.

11 Step forward with the right leg and bring the right arm underneath the left arm in front of the chest. Ensure that Juji Uke (x-block) is performed.

12 Step down into Migi Zenkutsu Dachi and block right Jodan Uke. The face must be protected at all times.

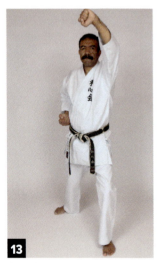

13 Step forward performing Jodan Uke with the left arm.

1st KIAI!

14 Step forward a third time performing right Jodan Uke and Kiai!

15 Stretch across with the left leg 225° bringing the left arm up high across the chest and the right arm across the stomach.

CHAPTER 7   Ipponme

16
Step down into Hidari Zenkutsu Dachi performing left Gedan Barai.

17
In the same direction, step forward punching right Junzuki.

18
Step across with the right leg 90° bringing the right arm up high across the chest.

19
Step down into Migi Zenkutsu Dachi performing right Gedan Barai.

20
Step forward in the same direction and punch left Junzuki.

21
Stretch across with the left leg 45° bringing the left arm up high across the chest.

71

Step down left Gedan Barai - Zenkutsu Dachi.

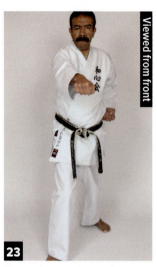
Step forward performing Migi Junzuki.

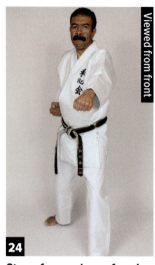
Step forward performing Hidari Junzuki.

Step forward performing Migi Junzuki and Kiai!

Stretch across with the left leg preparing to position the body at 225°.

Step down into Hidari Zenkutsu Dachi swinging the right arm all the way round and bringing the left hand underneath to perform Juji Uke.

CHAPTER 7　　Ipponme

28 Perform left Jodan Uke.

29 Step forward and punch Migi Junzuki.

30 Stretch across with the left leg preparing to take the body through a 270° turn.

31 Pivot round into Hidari Zenkutsu Dachi, swinging thee right arm all the way round and bring the left hand underneath to perform Juji Uke.

32 Perform left Jodan Uke.

33 Step forward and punch Migi Junzuki.

3rd KIAI!

34 Step forward and punch Hidari Junzuki and Kiai! Return left leg to Yoi position.

Pinan Shodan (Pinan Number 1)

Pin-an (this is how it should be pronounced) Shodan kata is usually performed as a second kata in most Wado-Ryu syllabuses. This is no exception with my own organisation.

1
Yoi position.

2
Transfer weight on to the right leg, dropping both arms to the right side.

3
Block Soto Uke with the left arm and raise the right arm in front of the face to protect it, palm facing outwards. The stance is Neko-Ashi Dachi.

CHAPTER 7   Pinan Shodan

4 Strike down with Tettsui (right bottom fist) twisting the hip at 90° and pulling the left arm in across the chest.

5 Punch with the left fist Jodan height pulling the left leg into Shizentai Dachi.

6 Step to the left, dropping both arms down to the left side.

7 Block right Soto-Uke protecting the face with the left arm, adopting right Neko-Ashi Dachi.

8 Strike down with left Tettsui, twisting the hips at 90° tucking the right arm across the chest.

9 Retract the right leg and punch right Jodan height, pulling the right leg into Shizentai Dachi.

10 Pivot on the ball of the left foot, retracting the right leg and dropping the right arm across the lower body.

11 Kick right Chudan Maegeri and block right Soto Uke Jodan at 180°.

11a side view

12 Place right leg down directly in front of left leg after completing the kick and then transfer weight onto the right leg as you pivot round 180° (Back to original position).

13 Perform Hidari Shuto Uke in left Neko-Ashi Dachi.

14 Step forward and perform Migi Shuto Uke in Neko-Ashi Dachi.

CHAPTER 7   Pinan Shodan

15

Step forward and perform Hidari Shuto Uke in Neko-Ashi Dachi.

1st KIAI!

16

Step forward into right Zenkutsu Dachi performing Yonhon Nukite with the right hand and KIAI!

17

Stretch across with the left leg preparing to position the body 225°.

18

Perform Hidari Shuto Uke in Neko-Ashi Dachi.

19

Step forward and perform Migi Shuto Uke

20

Stretch the right leg across preparing to position the body at 90°.

77

21 Perform Migi Shuto Uke in Neko-Ashi Dachi.

22 Step forward and perform Hidari Shuto Uke in Neko-Ashi Dachi.

23 Step across with the left leg preparing to position the body at 45o, bringing the right arm up underneath the outstretched left.

23a viewed from front

24 Perform Migi Soto Uke, twisting the upper body through 90° turn.

24a viewed from front

CHAPTER 7 — Pinan Shodan

25 Kick right Maegeri Chudan.

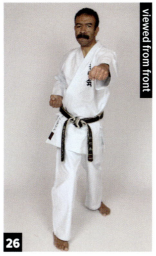

26 Place kicking leg down in front and perform left Gyakuzuki.

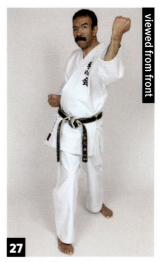

27 Block left arm Soto Uke on the spot, twisting the upper body through 90°.

28 Perform left Maegeri Chudan.

29 Snap leg back, placing it down in front and perform right Gyakuzuki.

30 Bring right leg in as close to left leg as possible, dropping both arms to the left.

31 Step forward with the right leg into right Zenkutsu Dachi and perform Migi Morote Uke KIAI!

32 Stretch across with the left leg, raising the arm across the chest, preparing to position the body at 225°.

33 Step down into left Zenkutsu Dachi, performing left Gedan Barai.

34 Step forward with right leg performing Juji Uke.

35 Place right foot down into Zenkutsu Dachi and perform right Jodan Uke.

36 Stretch across with the right leg, bringing the right arm up across the chest, positioning the body for a 90° turn.

CHAPTER 7 — Pinan Shodan

37 Step down into right Zenkutsu Dachi and perform right Gedan Barai.

38 Step forward and perform left Jodan Uke in left Zenkutsu Dachi.

39 Return to Yoi position.

Pinan Sandan (Pinan Number 3)

This Kata, like Pinan Nidan, has moves as close to the original ones devised by Anko Itosu.

1
Yoi position.

2
Step out to the left with the left leg, dropping left arm across the body and raising right arm high above the face.

3
Bring right arm forward, and start to raise left arm underneath.

CHAPTER 7   Pinan Sandan

4 Twist 90o into left Neko-Ashi Dachi, blocking left Soto Uke Jodan, pulling the right fist back onto the hip.

5 Step up into Heisoku Dachi with the right leg.

6 Bring the left arm down and the right arm up underneath into Juji Uke.

7 Perform left Chudan Gedan Barai and right Soto Uke Jodan.

8 Reverse the role of each arm.

9 Step out directly behind with the right leg.

10 Pivot round 180° into right Neko-Ashi Dachi performing right Soto Uke Jodan, pulling left hand back onto the hip.

11 Lower the right arm and raise the left arm up and underneath to perform Juji Uke.

12 Block left Jodan Soto Uke and right Chudan Gedan Barai.

13 Reverse the role of each arm.

14 Step to the left with the left leg, twisting the body into left Neko-Ashi Dachi at 90°.

15 Fully twist the hip and shoulder and perform left Soto Uke Jodan.

CHAPTER 7 — Pinan Sandan

16 Step forward into right Zenkutsu Dachi and strike the left arm with right Ude Uke (forearm strike).

17 Step up with the left leg into right Gyaku-Neko-Ashi-Dachi, bringing the right arm behind the left ear, fist clenched.

1st KIAI!

18 Strike right Uraken Jodan, pulling the left fist back onto the hip. KIAI!

19 Pivot around 180° into Musubi Dachi, placing both fists on the hip.

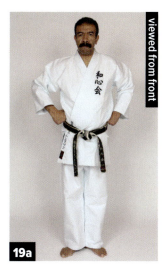

19a viewed from front

20 Cock the right fist as though about to punch forward, and step forward with the right leg. (viewed from front)

 **21** Land in Shiko Dachi and perform **Migi Empi Uke**, keeping both fists on the hip.	 **22** Strike right **Tettsui Uchi Chudan** level, remaining in Shiko Dachi.	 **22a**
 **23** Snap right arm back so the fist rests on the hip.	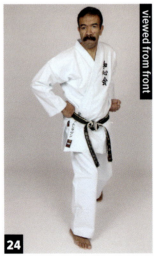 **24** Cock left fist onto hip and step forward with the left leg.	 **25** Land in Shiko Dachi, perform **Hidari Empi Uke Chudan**.

CHAPTER 7 Pinan Sandan

26 **26a**

Strike Hidari Tettsui Uchi Chudan.

27

Snap fist back.

28

Cock right fist onto hip and step forward with the right leg.

29

Perform Migi Empi Uke.

30

Strike Migi Tettsui Uchi Chudan and leave arm outstretched.

31. Step forward and punch left Junzuki and KIAI!

32. Perform Mikazuki Geri Uchi Chudan Level with the right leg, striking open left hand.

33. Pivot around 90° and strike open left hand with right Ude Uke.

34. Block down Morote Gedan Barai. Ensure both arms go past the body.

35. Block Morote Soto Uke Jodan. Again, ensure both arms go past the head.

36. Step to the left with the left leg pivoting 90o into left Neko-Ashi Dachi, crossing both arms, left arm underneath, in front of the face.

CHAPTER 7 — Pinan Sandan

37 Perform Morote Gedan Barai.

38 Perform Morote Soto Uke Jodan.

39 Both arms stretched out to the front, fists clenched.

40 Pull both hands back onto the hip and kick right Chudan Maegeri.

41 Land in Zenkutsu Dachi and punch right Junzuki.

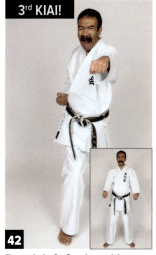
3rd KIAI!
42 Punch left Gyakuzuki, drawing the right leg in slightly and KIAI!. Draw front foot back in to Yoi position.

Pinan Yodan (Pinan Number 4)

1 Yoi position.

2 Transfer all the weight onto the right leg, dropping both arms down to the right hand side.

3 Block left open hand Haisho Jodan and bring the right open hand in front of the face for protection. Hidari Neko-Ashi Dachi.

4 Pull left leg in and step out with the right leg, dropping both arms down to the left hand side.

5 Block right Jodan Haisho Uke protecting the face with the left hand, right Neko-Ashi Dachi.

6 Pull the right leg in, so both heels are touching and both fists on the hip and begin to step forward with the left leg.

CHAPTER 7   Pinan Yodan

7 Step down into left Zenkutsu Dachi and perform Juji Uke Gedan, right arm on top of left.

8 Step forward with right leg into right Neko-Ashi Dachi, dropping both arms to the left.

9 Block Migi Morote Uke, keeping the upper body twisted at 90°.

10 Step up with the left leg into Heisoku Dachi, pulling the right arm down onto the hip and twisting the left arm across the body. Look to the left.

11 Kick left Maegeri Chudan 90° to the left at the same time executing a left Gedan Barai.

12 Snap the leg back, landing in left Zenkutsu Dachi and strike the open left arm with right Ude Uchi.

13
Pivot on the left foot 90°, pulling the right leg up into Heisoku Dachi, bring the left fist onto the hip and pull the right arm across the body. Look right.

14
Perform right Maegeri Chudan 90° to the right at the same time executing a right Gedan Barai.

15
Land in right Zenkutsu Dachi and strike the open right hand with left Ude Uchi.

16
Remaining in Zenkutsu Dachi, block front kick with an open handed Gedan Barai, bringing the right arm to protect the face.

17
Pivot round on the balls of the feet 90° and grab your opponent's punch with an open hand, simultaneously bringing the left hand up in font of the face.

18
Kick right Maegeri Chudan.

CHAPTER 7   **Pinan Yodan**

1st KIAI!

19
Snap the lg back and place it down, pulling the body forward into Gyaku-Neko-Ashi Dachi. The right arm comes round in a circular motion striking Uraken Jodan. The left hand comes down blocking Uraken Chudan, before returning to the left hip. KIAI!

20
Step out behind with the left leg preparing to turn 225°.

21
Block left Soto Uke Jodan in left Neko-Ashi Dachi.

22
Kick right Maegeri Chudan.

23
Land in right Zenkutsu Dachi and perform right Junzuki.

24
Punch left Gyakuzuki, pulling yourself into Gyakuzuki Dachi.

25 Step across with the right leg 90° into right Neko-Ashi Dachi and block right Soto Uke Jodan.

26 Kick left Maegeri Chudan.

27 Land in left Zenkutsu Dachi and perform left Junzuki.

28 Punch right Gyakuzuki into Gyakuzuki Dachi.

29 Step across with the left leg 45° into left Neko-Ashi Dachi, pulling both arms back to the right side of the body.

30 Perform Hidari Morote Uke Jodan.

viewed from front

CHAPTER 7 — Pinan Yodan

31 Step forward into right Neko-Ashi Dachi and perform **Migi Morote Uke Jodan**.

32 Step forward into left Neko-Ashi Dachi and perform **Hidari Morote Uke Jodan**.

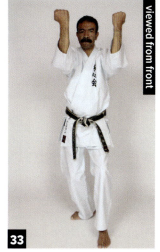

33 Push the right arm underneath the leg and perform **Morote Soto Uke Jodan**, ensuring that the blocks do not go wider than the shoulders.

34 Grab the opponent by the shoulders.

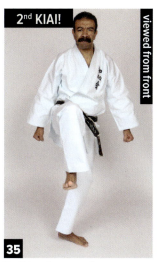

35 Pull both arms down open handed and raise the right knee. KIAI! (2nd KIAI!)

36 Place the right leg down, step out with the left leg, positioning yourself for a 225o turn. Raise the right hand and bring the left arm across the chest, with the left hand underneath the right armpit.

37 Pivot into left **Neko-Ashi Dachi**, blocking **Hidari Shuto Uke Jodan** and **Migi Teisho Uke Chudan**.

38 Push the right arm forward, placing the left arm underneath the left armpit. Stretch out with the right leg 90° to the right, placing the heel on the floor.

38a Close up of hand positions.

39 Pull yourself forward with the right leg into right **Neko-Ashi Dachi**, performing **Migi Shuto Uke Jodan**, and **Hidari Teisho Uke Chudan**.

40 Look directly in front and stretch out the left leg, pulling yourself back in to the Yoi position.

41 Yoi Position.

CHAPTER 7 — Pinan Godan

Pinan Godan (Pinan Number 5)

This is the only Pinan Kata that has slow movements as well as fast, explosive moves. All the techniques in the previous four Pinan Katas are performed at speed.

1 Yoi position

2 Look to the left. Step out to the left with the left leg into left Neko-Ashi Dachi, blocking left Soto Uke Jodan. Ensure the body is kept facing forward.

3 Punch right Gyakuzuki Chudan, twisting the hip 90o and retract the left leg slightly. Still remain in Neko-Ashi Dachi.

4
Drop the left heel and pull the right leg up to the left leg, so both heels touch in Musubi Dachi. Right fist slowly pulled onto right hip, left arm slowly placed across the chest. Perform slowly, Look right.

5
Step out to right with the right leg into right Neko-Ashi Dachi, blocking right Soto Uke Jodan. Ensure the body is kept facing forward.

6
Punch left Gyakuzuki Chudan, twisting the hip 90° and retract the right leg slightly. Still remain in Neko-Ashi Dachi.

7
Drop the right heel and pull the left leg up to the right leg, so both heels touch in Musubi Dachi. Left fist slowly pulled onto left hip, right arm slowly placed across the chest. Perform slowly.

8
Step forward with the right leg into Migi Neko-Ashi Dachi and block right Morote Uke Jodan. The body is twisted 90° to the attack, Mahanmi (long) Neko-Ashi Dachi.

9
Step forward with the left leg pulling both fists back onto the hip and as you land in left Zenkutsu Dachi, perform Juji Uke Gedan (X-block), right arm over the top of the left.

CHAPTER 7 — Pinan Godan

10 Pull both hands in and onto the chest. Rotating both wrists until palms face you.

11 Continue raising both arms opening the hands as they pace the face and rotate the wrists again so that the palms face outwards. Perform Juji Uke Jodan.

12 Bring the right hand up above the left hand and turn the palm of the right hand inwards.

13 Block with the back of the right hand, Morote Chudan Uraken Uke. The left hand reinforces the right.

14 Clench both fists and perform left Gedan Barai.

1st KIAI!

15 Step forward with the right leg and perform Junzuki Chudan and KIAI!

16 Pivot round on the ball of the left foot, raising the right arm, preparing to block an attack from behind.

17 Step down in Shiko Dachi and block right Gedan Barai against an attack delivered from behind.

17a side view

18 Raise both hands above the head, bringing the right hand underneath the left. Remain in Shiko Dachi stance.

19 Pull the left leg in towards the right and strike down with left Tettsui Uchi Chudan level, pulling the right fist back onto the hip.

20 Pivot on the ball of the left foot and step forward with the right leg into right Zenkutsu Dachi and strike the open left hand with right Ude Uchi, keeping the shoulders square.

CHAPTER 7 — Pinan Godan

21 Drop the right arm underneath twisting the upper body to the left and perform right Morote Soto Uke Jodan, twisting the body abruptly back to its original position. Simultaneously, pull the left leg up and stamp into right Gyaku-Neko-Ashi Dachi.

22 Drop the guard down into the stomach and duck quickly so you body is parallel to the floor.

23 Step out with your left leg into Junzuki No Tsukkomi Dachi and punch directly in front with the right hand, keeping the fist palm upwards. Look directly behind you and place your left fist on your chest.

23a side view

24 Pivot round on the left foot, raising the right leg as you spin 180°, preparing to jump in the air.

25 Jump as high as you can, tucking the legs up to avoid being struck. At the same time, pull both fists onto the hips.

26
Land in right Gyaku-Neko-Ashi Dachi, performing Juji Uke Gedan.

2nd KIAI!

27
Step out with the right leg to the right into Zenkutsu Dachi and perform Morote Soto Uke Jodan. KIAI!

side view

27a

28
Pull the left leg behind the right leg into Kokutsu Dachi, raising the left arm across the chest and dropping the right arm across the stomach as quickly as possible.

29
Simultaneously block Soto Uke Jodan with the right arm and left Gedan Barai remaining in Kokutsu Dachi.

30
Keep both arms perfectly still and pull the left leg up so the heels touch. Musubi Dachi.

CHAPTER 7 — Pinan Godan

31 Look 45° to the right.

32 Step forward at a 45° angle with the right leg into Kokutsu Dachi, bringing both arms across the chest, the left underneath the right.

33 Simultaneously block Soto Uke Jodan with the left arm and right Gedan Barai, remaining in Kokutsu Dachi.

34 Look in front, bend the right knee and return to the Yoi position.

CHAPTER 8

CHAPTER 8 — Pair Work

Yakusoku Kumite
(Pre-arranged pairs)

Pairs must be done with total commitment. Ensure that you are positioned directly in front of your opponent, whether on the offensive or defensive. Maintain good Ma-ai (distancing) especially the attacker and concentrate on your Kime (focussing). Where Tai-sabaki is involved in a technique then wait until a split second before the attack connects before shifting the body weight and counter-attacking.

The pairs shown should be carried out slowly and deliberately, gradually gaining speed with each repetition, until they are executed at full speed and power. The defender must respond to the attack to prevent injury.

The pairs shown may not necessarily be those included in your syllabus, however, I am sure some will be familiar. As Ippon Kumite techniques, they are all Wado-Ryu based and can be practised to complement your existing training programme. Both Tsuki (punches) and Keri (kicks) are covered in the Yakusoku Kumite chapter.

Yakusoku Kumite

Sometimes Tori and Uke are shown from the reverse side, in order to demonstrate the techniques in more detail.

Included in this chapter are various counters against different attacks. I have not limited it to the usual front punch and front kick techniques, but have included Mawashigeri and Sokuto. The last two pair techniques are Ohyo Gumite which are slightly more advanced than the Yakusoku Kumite and as close to free fighting as one can get.

1. 7 x Jodan Uke
2. 7 x Maegeri Uke
3. 4 x Mawashigeri Uke
4. 2 x Sokuto Uke
5. 2 x Ushirogeri Uke
6. 2 x Chudan Tsuki Uke
7. Ohyo Gumite Nos 2 and 3

These are two examples of Ohyo Kumite techniques as the techniques are slightly more advanced in application. The examples shown are Ohyo Kumite No 2 and Ohyo Kumite No 3.

It is essential that you bow before and after each pair technique depicted in Musubi Dachi. The attacker steps forward and the defender takes one step back simultaneously in every pair technique. Zanshin and Kime must be present at all times whilst practising these techniques.

Whenever Uke delivers a counter technique he must Kiai. With constant practice, all these pairs will become second nature.
Tori = Attacker
Uke = Defender

CHAPTER 8 — Jodan Uke 1

Both fighters face each other in left stance **(1)**.

(2) Tori steps forward and punches right Jodan Tsuki. Uke steps slightly to the left with his left leg and performs Taisabaki (hip shift), pulling his right leg across to the left, simultaneously pushing the punch aside with left Teisho (palm heel).

(3) Uke counters right Gyakuzuki to Tori's kidney/rib area and KIAI, ensuring his left Teisho is kept in place, snapping his fist back to the hip.

Both Tori and Uke take <u>one</u> pace backwards quickly, looking directly at each other, both ending up in opposite stance **(4)**. Finally, they both retract their front leg into Musubi Dachi and bow.

CHAPTER 8   Jodan Uke 2

Both fighters face each other in left stance **(1)**.

(2) Tori steps forward and punches right Jodan Tsuki. Uke steps to the right with his right leg and blocks Hidari Shuto Uke.

(3) Uke punches right Tsuki Jodan past Tori's head, retracting his left hand.

Both Tori and Uke take one pace backwards quickly, looking directly at each other, both ending up in opposite stance **(4)**.

CHAPTER 8 — Jodan Uke 3

Tori and Uke face each other in right stance **(1)**.

(2) Tori steps forward punching left Jodan Tsuki. Uke steps to the right with his right leg, dropping his left across his chest and blocks the punch with left Soto Uke.

(3) Uke punches with his right hand to Tori's left kidney, maintaining the left Soto Uke.

Both Tori and Uke take one pace backwards quickly, looking directly at each other, both ending up in opposite stance **(4)**.

CHAPTER 8 — Jodan Uke 4

1
Tori and Uke face each other in left stance.

2
Tori drops his right hand and throws right Haito Uchi, as the strike comes around, drops left arm across his chest.

3
Uke intercepts Tori's Haito with left Soto Uke.

4
Uke raises his right hand preparing to strike.

5
Uke strikes right Shuto, twisting his hips fully, to Tori's right collarbone.

6
Both Tori and Uke take one pace backwards into right stance.

CHAPTER 8 — Jodan Uke 5

1 Tori and Uke face each other in left stance.

2 Tori steps forward punching right Jodan Tsuki. Uke steps to the right raising his right hand, preparing to block.

3 Uke steps into Hidari Neko-Ashi, blocking right Soto Uke and striking Tori's bicep muscle.

4 Uke jumps into Shiko Dachi, striking right Tate Empi to Tori's ribcage.

5 Uke follows up by moving his right leg to the right and striking Hidari Ude retracting his right fist.

6 Both Tori and Uke take one pace backwards into left stance.

CHAPTER 8　　Jodan Uke 6

1 Tori and Uke face each other in right stance.

2 Tori steps forward punching left Jodan Tsuki. Uke steps out to the right with his right leg, pulling his left leg up in to **Neko-Ashi**, dropping his right arm across his chest and raising the left arm above his face.

3 Uke blocks Tori's punch with Hidari Shuto and strikes right Tettsui to Tori's ribs, Uke then grabs the wrist with his left hand and pull Tori forwards.

4 Uke delivers a left Mawashi Hiza to Tori's stomach.

5 Both fighters take one step back into opposite stance.

CHAPTER 8 — Jodan Uke 7

1 Tori left stance, Uke right stance.

2 Tori steps forward punching right Jodan Tsuki, Uke steps back blocking left Jodan Uke.

3 Uke whilst maintaining Jodan Uke, punches Gyakuzuki Chudan and immediately snaps the Gyakuzuki back.

4 As steps forward with his left leg, Uke intercepts using his right foot, as Tori throws a left Chudan Tsuki, Uke blocks right Shuto.

5 Uke steps down to the right and continues to push Tori's left arm behind him, Uke places his left arm across Tori's shoulders and drives down with the arm.

6 Maintaining the lock Uke delivers left Hiza Geri into Tori's stomach. Both fighters then take one step back into opposite stance.

CHAPTER 8 — Maegeri Uke 1

Both fighters face each other in left stance **(1)**.

(2) Tori kicks right Maegeri Chudan. Uke steps to the right with his right leg and blocks the attack with Hidari Teisho Uke.

(3) As Tori's weight falls forward, Uke throws a right Gyakuzuki Chudan, twisting his hip fully.

Both fighters take one step back into opposite stance **(4)**.

CHAPTER 8 — Maegeri Uke 2

1 Tori and Uke both in left stance.

2 Tori throws right Maegeri Chudan. Uke using Taisabaki with his right leg prepares to block with his left hand.

3 Uke completes the manoeuvre and as Tori's weight is dropping prepares to throw right Empi Uchi Jodan.

4 Uke delivers right Empi Uchi Jodan.

5 Uke takes one step back into right stance, Tori spins round into left stance.

CHAPTER 8 Maegeri Uke 3

1

Tori left stance, Uke right stance.

2

Tori kicks right Maegeri Chudan.

3

Uke jumps to the left, blocking the kick with **Migi Teisho Uke**.

4

Uke then throws left Gyakuzuki to Tori's right kidney.

5

Both fighters step back into left stance.

CHAPTER 8 — Maegeri Uke 4

1 Both fighters in left stance.

2 Tori steps forward Surikomi with his right leg. Uke prepares to block by raising his left arm across his chest.

3 Tori delivers a left Maegeri Chudan. Uke blocks down left Gedan Barai.

4 Uke then delivers right Gyakuzuki Chudan to Tori's left kidney.

5 Both fighters step back into right stance.

CHAPTER 8 | Maegeri Uke 5

1
Both fighters in left stance.

2
Tori steps forward Surikomi with his right leg. Uke prepares to block by raising his right hand high to the right.

3
Close up of the Migi Teisho Uke.

4
As Tori kicks left Maegeri Chudan, Uke pivots on his right foot bringing his left leg around in an anti-clockwise movement and blocks Migi Teisho Uke.

5
As Tori's weight lands forward, Uke delivers left Gyakuzuki to Tori's left kidney.

6
Both fighters step back into opposite stance.

CHAPTER 8 — Maegeri Uke 6

1 Both fighters in left stance.

2 Tori throws right Maegeri Chudan, Uke drags his right leg to the left with moving his left leg (Taisabaki).

3 As Tori completes his kick and his leg begins to descend, Uke quickly places his instep behind Tori's leg.

4 Uke extends Tori's right leg, breaking his balance.

5 Uke then delivers right Gyakuzuki to Tori's right kidney.

6 Both fighters step back into opposite stance.

CHAPTER 8 — Maegeri Uke 7

Tori left stance, Uke right stance **(1)**.

(2) Tori kicks right Maegeri Chudan. Uke steps to the left with his left leg and as Tori's kick is completed, Uke hooks his right leg behind Tori's descending leg. Uke continues to pull on the leg, breaking Tori's balance.

(3) Uke then throws left Gyakuzuki Chudan to Tori's right kidney.

Both fighters take one step back into left stance **(4)**.

CHAPTER 8 — Mawashigeri 1

1 Tori left stance, Uke right stance.

2 Tori throws right Mawashigeri Chudan, Uke steps forward, straight into Tori's attack, delivering a right front hand punch to Tori's stomach.

3 Uke immediately prepare to throw a left Furizuki (swing punch) and delivers the punch to Tori's sternum.

4 Uke snaps the Furizuki straight back to the hip leaving the right hand punch in the stomach.

5 Both fighters step back into left stance.

CHAPTER 8   Mawashigeri 2

1
Tori left, Uke right stance.

2
Tori prepares to throw right Mawashigeri Chudan. Uke steps in with his left leg so both his feet are close together.

3
As Tori's Mawashigeri is extended, Uke steps out with his left leg, blocking the kick at the thigh and begins to push out.

4
As Tori's balance is broken, Uke delivers a right Gyakuzuki Chudan.

5
Both fighters step back into opposite stance.

CHAPTER 8 — Mawashigeri 3

1 Both fighters in left stance. Tori throws Mawashigeri Jodan. Uke leans back and pushes the kick aside with his open left hand.

2 Uke delivers Mawashigeri Jodan with his right leg.

3 As Uke immediately places his right leg down, he grabs Tori's collar with his right hand and whilst stepping forward with his left leg, sweeps Tori's left leg with his right leg.

4 Uke pulls Tori to the floor, without letting go his collar.

5 Uke pins Tori with his left knee and delivers left Gyakuzuki Jodan.

6 Both fighters step back into opposite stance.

CHAPTER 8 — Mawashigeri 4

1
Both fighters in right stance. Tori steps forward with his left leg Surikomi.

2
Uke grabs Tori's right Mawashigeri Chudan from underneath, delivering a right hand stomach punch and immediately grabs Tori's collar after completing the punch.

3
Uke lifts upwards, breaking Tori's balance and sweeps Tori over his right leg.

4
As Tori goes down, Uke keeps the pressure on Tori's right leg (which he did not release) and pushes Tori's left leg out with his right leg.

5
Uke delivers right Gyakuzuki to Tori's sternum.

6
Uke throws Tori's leg away from him and both fighters return to left stance.

CHAPTER 8 — Sokuto Uke 1

1 Both fighters in right stance. Tori steps forward with his left leg Surikomi. Uke Steps to the left with his left leg, raising his right arm across his chest.

2 As Tori delivers a right Sokuto Chudan, Uke blocks right Gedan Barai.

3 As Tori's weight descends, Uke delivers left Gyakuzuki to Tori's right kidney.

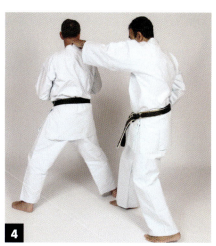

4 Uke immediately grabs Tori's collar with his left hand.

5 Uke pulls on the collar and sweeps Tori's right leg with his left.

6 As Tori goes down, Uke follows through, never letting go of the collar, pinning him with his right knee and delivering right Gyakuzuki Jodan. Both fighters return to left stance.

CHAPTER 8 — Sokuto Uke 2

1
Tori right stance, Uke left stance. Tori steps forward with his left leg Surikomi. Uke steps back with his left leg, raising both arms above his head in a circular motion.

2
As Tori's sidekick is extended, Uke blocks right Teisho Uke reinforced with his left hand on top.

3
As Tori's leg descends, Uke prepares to strike.

4
Uke jumps in, punching with his right hand to Tori's chest and simultaneously with his left hand, to the kidney.

5
Uke then steps forward with his left leg applying pressure with his right leg to Tori's right knee and swings his right arm across his chest.

6
Uke applying full pressure, drops Tori down onto one knee and strikes Migi Empi Uchi to the back of Tori's head. Both fighters step back into opposite stance.

CHAPTER 8 — Ushirogeri 1

1 Both fighters in left stance. Uke throws left lunge punch to the face. Tori leans back, pushing the punch aside with the left Shuto and steps across with his left leg.

2 Tori spins around and kicks right Ushirogeri Chudan. Uke steps to the left to avoid the kick and grabs it with his right arm, simultaneously grabbing Tori's collar with his left hand.

3 Uke places his right instep behind Tori's left knee and pushes down.

4 As Tori drops to the floor, Uke pushes down with his left hand.

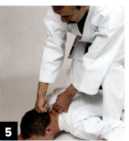

5 Uke then places his right knee in Tori's back and punches right Gyakuzuki Jodan.

6 Both fighters step back into left stance.

CHAPTER 8 — Ushirogeri 2

1
Tori right, Uke left stance. Tori brings his right leg across his body preparing to deliver Ushirogeri.

2
Tori delivers left Ushirogeri Chudan. Uke jumps to the right blocking the kick with left Gedan Barai.

3
As Tori's weight descends and he turns, Uke delivers left Haito Uchi Chudan.

4
Uke immediately turns the strike to a grab and pushes his left leg through Tori's legs.

5
Uke then lifts Tori up using his hip and throws him.

6
Tori falls face downwards and Uke pins him with his left knee and delivers right Gyakuzuki Jodan. Both fighters return to right stance.

CHAPTER 8 — Chudan Uke 1

1 Both in left stance.

2 Tori steps forward punching right Chudan Tsuki. Uke Taisabakis to the left and delivers left Jodan Tsuki.

3 Uke retracts his left leg.

4 Uke then delivers a Kingeri (groin kick) with his right foot.

5 Uke 'follows through' placing his right foot down in front.

6 Both fighters step back into left stance.

CHAPTER 8 Chudan Uke 2

1 Tori in left stance, Uke in right stance. Tori steps forward punching right Chudan Tsuki.

2 Uke steps back with his right leg pivoting on the ball of his left foot and blocks left Ude Uke.

3 UKe immediately delivers a left Uraken Chudan to Tori's stomach.

4 Uke then swings his right arm back, preparing to strike.

5 Uke then strikes right Haito to Tori's stomach.

6 Both fighters step back into opposite stance.

CHAPTER 8 — Ohyo Gumite 2

1 Both fighters in left stance. Tori steps forward punching right Jodan Tsuki. Uke steps to the right with his right leg pulling himself into left Neko-Ashi Dachi. He blocks the punch with left Uraken Uke and strikes Tori's stomach with right Haito.

2 Uke pulls both hand back onto his hip and then grabs Tori's arm from underneath.

3 Uke twists the arm over, grabbing the wrist and bicep.

4 Uke delivers right Ura-Mawashigeri Jodan, pulling Tori's arm.

5 Without Uke placing his kicking leg down, he sweeps Tori's right leg from him. As Tori descends, Uke pulls him in.

6 Uke places Tori's left elbow joint against his left leg, applying pressure, also pinning him with his right knee and then punches to the face with right Gyakuzuki. Both fighters step back into left stance.

CHAPTER 8 — Ohyo Gumite 3

1
Both fighters in left stance.

2
Tori steps forward punching right Jodan Tsuki. Uke Taisabakis to the left into Shiko Dachi and delivers Hidari Tettsui to Tori's ribcage.

3
Uke then moves his left leg to the left and raises his right arm preparing to strike.

4
Uke delivers right Tettsui to Tori's nape and immediately steps forward with his right leg keeping behind Tori.

5
Uke pivots on his right foot and sweeps Tori's left leg away from him using his own left leg.

6
As Tori descends, Uke follows him down and punched right Gyakuzuki Jodan.

Both fighters step back into opposite stance.

CHAPTER 9

 **CHAPTER 9**

Ji-Yu Kumite

Ji-Yu Kumite (free fighting) is the ultimate test of a karate-ka's skills. Attacking blocking and countering with all the techniques taught is not just a test of your physical prowess, but also your mental attitude towards others.

In Ji-Yu Kumite, trying to make controlled contact using many and various techniques with your opponent is very challenging and extremely rewarding when successful. The target area is limited and so are the permitted techniques. Even so, one still has a vast repertoire of technique to draw upon.

Kihon, Yakusoku-Kumite and Kata are essential preparatory training for Ji-Yu Kumite. The use of Kime, Ma-ai (distancing) and good Kokyu (breathing) are just as essential as speed and good technique. As a student progresses through the Kyu grades, then his/her fighting ability should do likewise. Through Ji-Yu Kumite a student's sense of awareness is greatly increased and his reactions to block, counter and attack become instinctive rather than rehearsed.

There are techniques in free fighting that are difficult to execute with control, yet still permitted. These must be practised regularly if you wish to include them in your repertoire. Kakato-geri (axe-kick) and Ushiro-mawashigeri (back spinning kick) are such techniques, but when used correctly, are very spectacular. Sankaku-geri (triangular kick) is the ultimate kicking technique. This is where three different powerful kicks are delivered whilst jumping. Ashi-barai (sweeping) is encouraged in Wado-Ryu and many advanced sweeps are now included in karate tournaments.

A good attitude must always be predominantly in one's fighting, as without it severe injury could easily be caused. The Japanese word for a good fighting spirit is 'Toh Kon'. Techniques that are not allowed in Ji-Yu Kumite are those that could easily maim, cause loss of sight, or even kill. For example: Nukite (spear hand) or any other open handed techniques to the face; Kansetsu-geri (joint kicks) and Kingeri (groin kick). The last technique is not usually allowed but certain schools allow its use as long as a groin guard is worn.

As with all the other stages in karate, when first starting Ji-Yu Kumite as a low kyu grade, at least 7th kyu, it should be done slowly with a senior grade. This will allow you to practise your attacks and blocks and be corrected where necessary. In free fighting, it is always best to put combination attacks together rather than try and hit your opponent with a single technique. This is quite obvious, for if you should miss, or have your technique blocked, you may be subject to a counter attack.

With a higher grade the chances of any self-inflicted injury are greatly reduced. The majority of injuries that do occur when first staring Ji-Yu Kumite practice are to the fingers and toes. This is due to several factors. It takes time to clench a fist properly, squeezing all the air out and keeping the thumb tucked in. Pulling the toes back for front kick does not come naturally to many students. When it comes to implementing punches and kicks against an opponent, even if the techniques are applied correctly, the body may react against the impact.

It takes time to build up resistance. This is why it is essential that the fundamentals are fully grasped and a reasonable degree of fitness has been achieved before commencing Ji-Yu Kumite. As stated in the Preface, an instructor has a tremendous responsibility to his students. He should never allow them to fight too early, or even fight at all under certain circumstances. Example: the student's age must be taken into account as well as any injury or illness. It is also the instructor's responsibility to vet students by questionnaire about their medical history, before permitting them to start karate. Remember, you are never compelled to fight.

By starting in the manner I have suggested, Ji-Yu Kumite can be enjoyed in the same way as Kihon and Kata. However, if a hatred or phobia builds up against fighting possibly due to an unpleasant incident, then the rest of your karate will suffer and no progress will be made.

Competition Karate

The introduction of Competition Karate has allowed a martial art to become a sport. It must be stressed that this is not the only aspect of karate to have as one's goal. Nevertheless, karate tournaments are most exciting to watch, especially when the standard of the competitors is high. Students should always be encouraged to compete in either kata or kumite, but preferably both. It is not only a chance to put all those hours of dojo training to the test, but also a test of one's character in both success and defeat. In one day the student who has never witnessed any other form of karate may see several other styles of karate performing. Hopefully, a competitor will always leave a tournament having learnt something and enjoyed the experience. The successful are usually rewarded well and if one is winning consistently, then international competition is the next obviously step.

England has produced many excellent Wado-Ryu competition karate-ka, the best in the world, and hopefully will continue to do so.

CHAPTER 10

CHAPTER 10

The Name Wado Ryu

Hironori Ohtsuka deliberately set out to make Wado-Ryu a purely Japanese style of karate. He specifically discarded any form of technique that he found impractical and added as much of his Shindo Yoshin Ryu Ju-jutsu as possible, knowing that this was an inherent Japanese martial art.

Even the name Wado was purely Japanese. When asked to give the origins of his school of karate for a martial arts festival held in Kyoto during the 1930's, Ohtsuka merged the name of the founder of Shindo Yoshin with the name Wado Ryu. He originally named his style Shinshu Wado Ryu Ju-jutsu. He then dropped Shinshu as he was advised that both 'Wa' and 'Shinshu' stood for Japan. 'Wa' is usually accepted as only meaning 'peace'.

A further acceptance of Wado Ryu being a totally Japanese school of karate was the fact that most headmasters of Japanese martial arts assumed he had taken 'Wa' from the word 'Showa'. When Hirohito became the Emperor of Japan this period was called the Showa era (1926 – 1989). The period before this was the Meiji era (1867 – 1912). The Showa era was seen as the start of an era of peace and harmony. Again 'Wa' is seen as meaning both Japan and peace.

Whether it was the political climate in the late 1920s and early 1930s, or the fact that Ohtsuka felt that any martial art originating in another country was inferior, we will never know. But Ohtsuka's determination to make Wado Ryu karate a purely Japanese martial art was quickly accepted. This is acknowledged by the fact that Hironori Ohtsuka was awarded the rank of 'Jun-Go-To' and received the 'Sokokyoku-jitsu-Sho' medal by the Emperor of Japan in 1972. Ohtsuka was the first karate master to receive his 10th Dan from the Kokusai Budo In (International Martial Arts Federation).

AFTERWORD

I hope this book will be of assistance to students of all schools of karate, even though it is primarily aimed at students of either Wado Ryu, Wado Kai, or schools that base themselves on Wado.

I believe Karate's growth in the UK over the last five decades is due to many schools making an effort to mix with each other and as a consequence learn more about each other's styles. A karate-ka who has reached the level of fourth kyu, no matter what style, should have achieved a good foundation on which to build more advanced techniques. This book should help strengthen these foundations. Hopefully, a strong character, as well as good self-discipline, should start to emerge from a karate-ka who has reached the half-way mark on the kyu ladder.

It must always be remembered books are only aids and karate can never be learnt from books alone. There is absolutely no substitute for dojo training with a good Sensei.

Read on for a preview of Chris Thompson's new book, 'Fighting Spirit' – An autobiography.

FIGHTING SPIRIT
Karate - My Way of Life

by Chris Thompson
with Bill Taylor

On a hot and sticky summer evening in 1969, just as the Apollo space crew were making their final preparations to land on the Moon, I walked into a martial arts dojo for the first time. Strictly speaking, the house rules of the Judokan in west London said I was too young at fifteen to join their beginners' karate class. Children were not allowed in karate dojo at the time and women were actively discouraged. But they signed me up anyway and so began the adventure of my lifetime. The instructor with the black belt round his waist that night, Bob Wignall, had served his time working as a fairground bare knuckle boxer before taking up karate. As you might imagine, he was tough and strong and powerful, but he also turned out to be humble and courteous. Despite his hard fairground past, I never heard him swear. He was in every sense a gentleman.

No one spoke at all in the dojo: total discipline, total silence. I was the youngest in the class, a tall skinny black kid from West London. Watching from the shadows were some of the first generation of Japanese judo and karate masters who had moved to Britain to teach their fighting arts in the West. By the time I sat the test for my first karate grading a few months later, almost all the adult students in that beginners' class had disappeared. The training was too tough. But I suspected I had found my destiny – my way. There was just an aura of magic about it. I was star struck. After more than forty-five years of teaching karate all over the world, the magic is still with me and I realise that I have had a lucky life.

It didn't look that way a few years earlier when a freak accident left me blind in one eye. Just three months into my first year at secondary school, I was messing around with a friend in the garden at home in Maida Vale, London. We put some potassium permanganate, Andrews Liver Salts and a little bit of everything into a screw-cap bottle and shook it up. There was an almighty explosion and I was left with a massive chunk of glass in my right eye. I was holding the bottle in my right hand and I'm lucky not to have lost my hand as well. I don't remember feeling any pain at all, but when my mother came running out she found me with my T-shirt completely covered in blood.

Throughout November 1965, I spent a month in the Western Ophthalmic Hospital in London's Marylebone Road and the surgeons fought hard to save my right eye. At one stage they were quite happy and hopeful that my sight would return. But not long after I left hospital and went back to Christopher Wren High School, one of the school thugs was doing the rounds of the playground flicking rubber bands at the faces of other students. He hit me in the injured eye and in an instant completely tore apart all the painstaking work the surgeons had done to give me back full sight. For the rest of my life, I was blind in my right eye.

PINAN NIDAN VARIATIONS

The Wado-Ryu Karate Do Renmei of Japan perform Pinan Nidan differently to the kata shown. The main differences are at the beginning and end of the kata. It is assumed that Hironori Ohtsuka blended the karate-jutsu techniques he learnt from Funakoshi with his Ju-jutsu knowledge to arrive at the moves which make this following version of Pinan Nidan peculiar to Wado-Ryu.

Starting off in Yoi position:

2. Raise the left arm above the head, taking all the weight onto the right leg, bringing the right arm across the chest.
3. Block Hidari Tettsui (hammer fist), at the same time pulling the right fist on to the right hip, going into Hidari Neko-Ashi Dachi. It is important to keep the body square to the front.
4. Step forward punching Migi Junzuki (as in previous kata)
5. Pull right leg back behind you, placing right fist on to chest
6. Twist 180 and block Migi Gedan Barai in Migi Junzuki Stance
7. Retract right leg, bringing right arm across the body before raising above the head
8. Block Migi Tettsui in Migi Shizentai-Dachi (natural stance)
9. Step forward punching Hidari Junzuki (as in previous kata)

All the moves from this point are identical to moves 8-24 in the previous kata

26. Stretch across with the left leg, preparing to position the body at 225
27. Pivot into Hidari Neko-Ashi Dachi, placing the left hand in Nukite position, palm upwards, on top of the right hand, also in Nukite position, palm downwards
28. Slide left leg forward into Shiko-Dachi and strike Hidari Nukite to your opponent's kidney, the right hand is placed across the stomach
29. Pivot on the balls of the feet, placing the right hand, palm up on top of the left hand, palm down
30. Step forward into Migi Shiko-Dachi and strike Migi Nukite
31. Pull the right leg across 90, raising both arms
32. Place the right hand, Nukite position palm upwards, on top of the left hand, Nukite position palm downwards, as you step into Migi Neko-Ashi-Dachi
33. Slide the right leg forward striking Migi Nukite
34. Pivot on the balls of the feet, placing the left hand, palm upwards, on top of the right hand palm downwards
35. Step forward with the left leg and strike Hidari Nukite
36. Retract the left leg, crossing both arms to return back to Yoi position

Appendix | Variations

2

3

4

5

6

7

26

27

28

Appendix | Variations

PINAN SANDAN VARIATIONS

Like Pinan Nidan Kata the Pinan Sandan of Wado-Ryu Karate Do Renmei varies considerably from Itosu's original moves. However, it is very similar to the Heian Sandan of Shotokan. Ohtsuka, it would seem, did not vary the Kata too greatly from the way it was taught by Gichin Funakoshi, although his form differs greatly to that of Ankoh Itosu. There is no confirmed proof that Funakoshi ever learnt the Pinan Kata directly from Itosu and that his versions were a mixture of his own interpretations, along with the moves he picked up from other students of Itosu.

The main differences in the Kata are at the end, where the practitioner is attacked from behind.

Moves 75-87 are identical to the previous kata shown.

16. Step forward into Migi Junzuki, performing Migi Nukite Chudan
17. Pull the left leg across behind and twist the upper body 180 grabbing the opponent's guard with the right hand.
18. Pull your opponent down, symbolised by slapping the back of the right hand on the back of the right thigh. The body has completely twisted 180 and is leaning forward at a 45 angle.
19. Pull the left leg around 180, crossing both arms in front of the chest.
20. Step down into Shiko-Dachi and strike Hidari Tettsui Chudan.
21. Step forward with the right leg and perform Migi Junzuki Kiai.

Here the kata is exactly the same as moves 91 to 106 in the previous kata.

32. Step up, keeping the same height, with the right leg into Kiba Dachi, keeping the arms perfectly still.
33. Step across with the left leg, preparing to turn 180.
34. Twist the body completely round into Shizentai Dachi and strike Hidari Empi Chudan, simultaneously wrapping the right arm around the face, punching Migi Seiken Jodan. (Your opponent grabs you from behind and you slam your left elbow into his stomach and right fist into his face.)
35. Step out to the right with the right leg.
36. Transfer the weight onto the right leg into Shizentai Dachi and reverse the role of each arm i.e. right elbow into the stomach, left fist into the face.
37. Drop both arms down to return to Yoi position.

Appendix   Variations

 16
 17
 18
 19
 20
 21
 33
 34
 35
 36